IMAGES
of Canada

SAINT JOHN

MORE POSTCARD MEMORIES

On July 28, 1937, Harry H.Richardson (left) and Stanley LeBlanc (right) proudly displayed the 605-pound tuna they caught at Bliss Harbor, Charlotte County, earlier that day. LeBlanc was a deep-sea fishing expert and Richardson an avid enthusiast of the sport that both were promoting as an attraction for tourists.

The tuna had wandered into a big weir at Bliss Harbor and began to feast on herring and other fish caught in the weir. Chief Inspector McLeese got word of this and reported to the deep-sea angling club members. After one unsuccessful attempt, a party of four, Stanley LeBlanc, Harry Richardson, Max Marcus, and C.R. Wasson returned to the battlefield two days later. At 10 a.m., the "horse mackerel" was sighted by LeBlanc as the men cruised the waters of Bliss Harbor in a small dory. He lashed out with his harpoon that had been borrowed from the New Brunswick Museum and succeeded in spearing the big fish. The battle was on! The boat was spun around and towed madly through the waters for more than an hour when the tuna finally fought its way to shore. During the battle an adjacent fishing party including Inspector McLeese and Detective Kilpatrick, were among the watchers on shore. When the tuna came ashore, Detective Kilpatrick apparently ended its life with seven shots from a .303 rifle; but the fighting spirit of the tuna carried it 30 feet along the shore before it finally recognized defeat.

With their catch on the back of a truck, they returned to Saint John, stopping on King Street near the studio of Harry Richardson, a photo engraver by trade. At the request of eager onlookers, they suspended the tuna from a power pole for a time before packing it in ice and placing it on display in the window of the National Packing Co., Ltd., on Union Street.

Cover: Pictured is the Transportation Festival Parade in 1935. Above the Primrose Gas Station, K.C. Irving observes the parade from his office window. In 1998 he was selected by historians as Canada's greatest entrepreneur of the 20th century.

IMAGES
of Canada

SAINT JOHN
MORE POSTCARD MEMORIES

Terry R.J. Keleher and Donald P. Collins

ARCADIA

Published by Arcadia Publishing,
an imprint of Tempus Publishing, Inc.
2 Cumberland Street
Charleston, SC 29401

Printed in Great Britain.

Library of Congress Catalog Card Number: 98-87698

For all general information contact Arcadia Publishing at:
Telephone 843-853-2070
Fax 843-853-0044
E-Mail arcadia@charleston.net

For customer service and orders:
Toll-Free 1-888-313-BOOK

Visit us on the internet at http://www.arcadiaimages.com

CONTENTS

The staff of the Purity Ice Cream Co. Ltd. pose for a picture in front of their newly built ice cream plant at 92–98 Stanley Street in this 1920 photograph. The business was started by Adolf Stearn who managed it until 1925 when J. Frank Tilley took over. That year, the company resided at 113 City Road and apparently maintained both locations until being taken over by Dealer's Dairy in 1933.

ACKNOWLEDGMENTS

We wish to thank the people whose assistance made this book possible. In no particular order, they are: the staff of the Regional Library, David Goss, Richard Thorne, Don Armstrong, Doug Gould, Andrew Colwell, Rev. Thomas Graham, Gerry Taylor, Jean Mahaney, Bill Bailey, Peter Larocque, Capt. Francis Quinn, Bill Giggey, Bobby Ring, Robert McDevitt, Gail Nealey, R. Whidden Ganong, Ron Park, Susan Trites, Carey Ryan, Rev. Stuart Allan, Paul Hill, Glen Stewart and Frank McNeill & the Royal Canadian Legion, Mitchell Carr, Jean Cail, Vincent Galbraith, and Rob Roy and Boyd Trites for photographic development.

For photo credit, (T for top of page and B for bottom of page): Byron O'Leary (B p.128), Ron Grant (B p.66, B p.73), Bob Boudreau (B p.72), Dan Dineen (B p.71), Byron Wood (T p.73), Arthur Gould (B p.79, T p.80, B p.80), Catherine Somerville (B p.116), Joan Stoney (T p.53, T p.78, T p.83, T p.85), The New Brunswick Museum (B p.17, T p.18, B p.18, T p.19, B p.19, T p.123), Public Archives of Canada (T p.66), Saint John Harbour Commissioners Annual Report 1929 (B p.51, T p.65, B p.65, T p.71), Portland United Church (p.81), N.B. Protestant Orphanage Foundation (B p.92), and St. Malachy's High School (B p.113).

A special debt of gratitude is owed those real photo artists whose postcard studies provided a unique close-up of the times. They are: Isaac Erb, D. Smith Reid, Harry H. Richardson, Harold Climo, L.M. Harrison, and all the other artists whose work was unsigned. A special note goes to the local companies who produced many of the great images we used: E.G. Nelson, J. & A. MacMillan, and Saint John News.

The many large companies that produced postcards that were of the printed variety rather than real-photographic quality were: Valentine and Sons, Warwick & Rutter, Decor, Photogelatine Engraving, and the New Brunswick Tourist Association.

Don Collins, an exceptional postcard collector, has again provided many wonderful photographic postcard images to make this book a reality. A special thanks to our typist and editor-in-chief, Irene Keleher for her constant support and her usual superb job.

INTRODUCTION

Saint John In The Golden Age of Postcards, our first book, used the era, 1900 to 1915, to lay a historical foundation of the city through captioned postcard views. We have attempted to continue our quest by looking at the city again through our own personal collections and any other additions that are gratefully acknowledged in the text.

We are attempting to revisit a Saint John mainly of the pre-1950 era through the important events of this period, without reviewing the postcard concepts and understandings stated in our first book, which focused on an overall historical view of the city.

The image that Saint John presented at the beginning of the 20th century through a patriotic fervour captured in crested postcards is no longer of great importance. However, you will find the real photograph image of this more contemporary period taking over from printed lithographic views. The real photograph image was a better way to present special events, disasters, and the ordinary lives of Saint Johners at this time.

By the end of World War I printed postcards were not as colourful as they had been prior to the beginning of the war. Germany's great quality printing techniques, use of colour, and sharpness were no longer available due to the circumstances of the war. At this time many printed postcards featured white borders, and this helps date them as being after WW I.

We made every possible effort to state the names of companies that published these postcards in the acknowledgments section. Further, individual postcard photographers are also listed in this section.

More Postcard Memories will attempt to have an impact on the memories of our senior citizens of Saint John. It is our intention and hope that these rekindled reminiscences will be shared with their families and friends as they enjoy these eventful-captioned images. In this spirit we humbly dedicate this book to those who actually lived in and can share these times from their own experiences.

This is the Purity Ice Cream Co. Ltd. at the Stanley Street location in 1920. Parked in front of the business was the company's "fleet" of delivery vehicles, which included five trucks and three horse-drawn wagons. When the company opened in 1920 it advertised "the finest grades of Ice Cream, Ices & Sherbets." Note the illustration of the ice cream "brick" on the side of the truck. Many will remember ice cream being commonly sold in this fashion well into the 1960s.

One

WORLD WAR I

Our first book concluded with the early portion of the First World War, focusing on the departure of the famous "Fighting 26th Battalion." While the 26th was the most celebrated unit associated with Saint John, there were several others that became near and dear to the community. In this chapter we present some of the other military units which, whether their stay in the city was a few weeks or several months, managed to weave their way into the fabric of the city. It must be remembered that at that time soldiers were looked upon with great reverence, respect, and awe; indeed, they were considered heroes. They were heroes in every sense of the word when one considers the thousands who volunteered with the knowledge that many of them would not return alive.

The 52nd, 69th, 115th, and 140th Battalions, along with the 4th Overseas Siege Battery, are just some of the units, local or otherwise, that called Saint John home during the war. They played hockey and baseball with the locals, attended church and other social events, and spent much of their spare time within the community making new friends. These groups were immortalized on film as seen on these postcards produced by local photographers, including D. Smith Reid, noted for capturing the views of the 26th Battalion.

Our first view shows a large throng of local citizens who have gathered to bid farewell to the "boys," some of whom can be seen in the foreground.

The embarkation of the 52nd Battalion, which took place on November 23, 1915, is depicted on these postcards. The 52nd consisted of 40 officers and 1,032 men, and they were accompanied by the 9th Regiment Mounted Rifles, whose compliment included 27 officers and 559 men. Another 203 officers and men from smaller units also joined them on the transport *California*. The 52nd Battalion was from Ontario, based in Port Arthur. Although their stay in Saint John was brief, just 16 days, they nonetheless were treated royally while in the city and had nothing but happy memories of their time spent. On the day of their departure they, along with the 9th Mounted Rifles, marched from the Armoury to Long Wharf through streets lined with well-wishers.

An unidentified company of soldiers appears on these two postcards, marching on Charlotte Street near the head of King. Soldiers marching through the streets of Saint John were a common sight during the war years. The City Market can be seen in the background along with F.W. Daniels on the left, later Woolworth's, which is now the location of a bargain shop. Also prominent in these 1916 views is one of the city's old streetcars. This is car #84, which was one of the two cars that were attacked at Market Square during the infamous streetcar riot of July 24, 1914.

On March 30, 1916, the No. 4 Overseas Siege Battery assembled on King Street East for an unofficial final inspection by the local citizens, as seen in the two views shown here. Being stationed on Partridge Island, the men crossed from the West Side on the ferry and after landing they marched to King Street East. Many photographs were taken by professional and amateur alike while the men stood at attention. Afterwards, they assembled in front of the bandstand in King Square to listen to a stirring address delivered by Mayor Frink. Following this, they attended the Imperial Theatre where they watched motion pictures of local units that had been made a few weeks previously.

This is another view of the No. 4 Overseas Siege Battery on King Street East. The men lined up with officers in front, facing family, friends, and other well-wishers. The following day, the men boarded a train bound for Halifax amidst another large crowd at Union Station. On April 5, they were among some six thousand troops that boarded the White Star liner *Olympic* (sister ship to the ill-fated *Titanic*), which was used as a military transport during the war.

On November 27, 1915, the 69th Battalion arrived in Saint John at Union Station aboard two trains that had arrived that morning. This French-Canadian unit was from the Montreal area and came to Saint John to continue their training whilst they filled out their ranks. After a warm welcome from Mayor Frink, they began the march from Union Station to the Armoury.

After leaving Union Station the 69th Battalion marched up Mill Street, down Dock to Market Square, and then up to the head of King where they turned right onto Charlotte on their way to the Armoury. It was at the head of King Street that D. Smith Reid had his camera set up where he captured the four views on this and the following page. In the first shot, an automobile bearing Mayor Frink and the 69th's commanding officer, Lt.Col. J.A. Dansereau, leads the men on their way. Below, the 69th's regimental band reaches the head of King while the crowds that had gathered look on. Notice streetcar #73 which, forced to pause while the battalion passed, afforded its passengers front row seats.

The procession continues and a group of boys have apparently joined the 69th in the parade past the camera. When the 69th Battalion arrived in Saint John, there was some nine hundred men in the unit. Some of the latest recruits either had not been issued uniforms yet or had uniforms that were incomplete. In the lower view a number of men are still wearing civilian hats. The 69th would spend the winter in Saint John before leaving for England on April 17, 1916, on board the transport *Scandinavian*. While here, the battalion formed a strong bond with the local citizens. One example was the men of Company "B" who presented an ornate shield to the Germain Street Baptist Church as a token of their appreciation for the friendship and hospitality that had been extended to them.

A portion of the 115th Battalion assembled in front of Germain Street Baptist Church. The 115th was a New Brunswick battalion with many local men in its ranks. "A" Company consisted entirely of men from Saint John. While in the city they were quartered at the Exhibition buildings. On June 13, 1916, they were presented with both the King's and Regimental Colors by Lt. Gov. Wood during a ceremony held at Seaside Park.

Here the 115th is shown on the Exhibition grounds with the Armoury in the background. They were known as "Wedderburn's Warriors," after their commanding officer, Lt. Col. F.V. Wedderburn, one of the best-known and respected men in the city. On the morning of June 19, 1916, the 115th left by train for Valcartier Camp in Quebec where they would continue their training for overseas duty.

The 140th Battalion was another New Brunswick unit that boasted no less than 21 officers plus 348 N.C.O.s and men from Saint John. Commanded by Lt. Col. L.H. Beer, they were known as the "St. John Tigers" and were quartered at the old immigration building in West Saint John. In this view on St. John Street, the men have paused in front of Queen Square West. The 140th left for Valcartier on June 22, 1916.

The H.M.S. *Dragon*, at anchor in Saint John harbour, fires a royal salute as the pinnace bearing Edward, Prince of Wales, heads for the landing at Reed's Point on August 15, 1919. The pinnace is just coming into view to the right of the tugboat *Kenton*, which is loaded to capacity with onlookers there to witness the Prince's arrival.

After the pinnace arrived, the Prince stepped onto the landing and came up a short flight of stairs, where he was officially welcomed to Canada by the governor general, the Duke of Devonshire. Although the day was overcast with persistent showers, it failed to dampen the spirits of the Prince or the thousands of local citizens on hand to greet him to the Loyalist City.

This is a scene at Reed's Point where 12 young ladies dressed in white appeared before the Prince carrying shields representing the various provinces and territories as well as Saint John. Identified in the photograph from left to right are: Dorothy Blizzard (Yukon), Ethel Powell (Ont.), Elizabeth Foster (N.B.), Rhonda Lloyd (Saint John), Alice Hayes (N.S.), Catherine McAvity (Sask.), Grace Kuhring (B.C.), Jean Anderson (Alta.), Ines Ready (Que.), Kathleen Stardee (N.W.T.), Ollie Golding (P.E.I.), and obscured behind Miss Foster was Phyllis Kenney (Man.).

18

After the festivities at Reed's Point concluded, the Prince entered an open car for a parade through the city. Here, the Prince's car pauses at King Square South where a striking incident took place. An elderly man who had taken part in the welcome to the late King Edward VII who visited here in 1860, pressed forward asking to shake the Prince's hand. Although initially restrained, the Prince requested he come forward, whereupon the two shook hands heartily amidst a rousing cheer.

The parade ended at the Armoury, where Prince Edward was to present the King's and regimental colors to the 26th Battalion. Before presenting the colors, he gave an address in which he spoke fluently on the exploits of the battalion during the war. In this view Lieutenant Ritchie of the 26th receives the King's colors from the Prince. Following this he presented the regimental colors to Lt. Armstrong.

Before presenting the colors, the Prince inspected the returned soldiers, who were arranged on the grounds in the form of a hollow square. Roughly three hundred former members of the 26th Battalion attended the event. Many wore their old uniforms, but the hats they wore were made especially for this occasion. Prince Edward is shown here during the inspection, accompanied by a group of officers with the Armoury in the background.

On the evening of June 10, 1925, the war memorial in King Square was unveiled in a ceremony held before 12,000 citizens. The memorial, a tribute to the soldiers who lost their lives in WW I, came about because of a movement initiated by the Imperial Order of the Daughters of the Empire. Spoon Island granite was used for the monument that stands 34 feet tall.

Two

STORMY WEATHER

With memories of the January 1998 ice storm still fresh in our minds, we will travel back in time to the early 1920s to look at two of the severest winter storms to hit the Saint John area in recorded history. On February 5 and 6, 1920, a crippling snow and ice storm struck the city and outlying areas. Power and telephone service was lost for, in many cases, several days. Railway and local streetcar service was badly disrupted and, over a week later, had not fully recovered. Telephone poles snapped like matchsticks under the strain of all the ice, and thousands of trees were destroyed or badly damaged.

In December 1922 and January 1923, a series of five snow storms occurred in rapid succession capped off by a severe blizzard on January 12 and 13. The city was still digging out as a result of the previous storms when this storm delivered a devastating blow. The winds created drifts of about 8 to 12 feet in height. Although power and telephone service was not affected, transportation of all sorts was brought to a virtual standstill.

Local photographer D. Smith Reid captured some of the results of the 1920 ice storm on film with a series of real-photo postcards, including the one above taken in King Square looking towards Charlotte Street. A heavy coat of snow and ice can be seen on the trees as the steeple of the Trinity Church towers over the buildings on Charlotte Street in the background.

With the bandstand behind him and the Tilley Monument on the right, a well-dressed man approaches Charlotte Street from King Square. Evidence of the storm can be seen with the ice-laden trees and their bent and broken branches. Many of these relatively young-looking trees are no doubt some of the more mature trees currently standing in the Square. This year (1998) those trees lost more branches to the ice.

This shot of King Square, like all the others, was taken the day after the storm. It was taken from Charlotte Street, a little to the right of the previous view. A woman can be seen walking southward towards the Dufferin Hotel. The bandstand and Tilley Monument are again in the background, partially obscured by the trees and their icy burden.

Above is a panoramic view of King Square taken from a nearby rooftop on Charlotte Street. The Square is covered by a blanket of snow topped with ice, and the bent and broken limbs of the trees are very much in evidence. On the upper right can be seen the old Presbyterian Church. Although no longer used as a church, the building still stands today, minus its steeple.

This shot was taken in King Square looking towards King Square South. The woman and child on the lower right are approaching the corner, with the Dufferin Hotel barely visible in the background. The building on the far left is the Imperial Theatre. In the foreground, we have an excellent example of a tree straining under the burden of snow and ice, and it is very reminiscent of what we saw this past January (1998).

Here is another view in King Square taken from the Charlotte Street side looking towards King Square South. The Tilley Monument and Imperial Theatre are very prominent in this shot. Again the trees can be seen with their limbs badly bent over, many of which were touching the ground. If you look closely at the large tree behind and to the left of the Tilley Monument, you will see one of its upper branches lying over the wires.

This shot was taken from the bandstand looking directly at the Imperial Theatre. To the left of the Imperial was I. Chester Brown's Dry Goods & Ladies' Wear, and next to Brown's was Lansdowne House, which was one of the many hotels in the King Square area. To the right of the Imperial was the Cash and Carry Store, which would be torn down a few years later to make way for the Admiral Beatty Hotel. The larger tree in the foreground, looking a little the worse for wear, still stands today.

The damage to the trees is severe in this view of the Old Loyalist Burial Ground. The tower in the background was part of the old police station, which sat on King Street East. To the left of the police station was the old No. 1 Fire Station. Today, with both stations gone, along with most, if not all, of the older trees, only the old headstones remain.

This is the first card showing the aftermath of the 1923 blizzard. It was taken from the eastern side of Coburg Street looking up towards the corner of Coburg and Carleton Streets. The old Starr residence can be seen at the head of the street, partially obscured by the snow and trees. The tree on the far right is still standing.

Here is another view of the huge snowdrifts left behind by the storms of early January 1923, this time on Wellington Row. St. John's [Stone] Church on Carleton Street is partly hidden behind the high bank of snow, with the Jewish Synagogue visible to the left. The buildings on the right, including those that housed the Imperial Optical Company, are no longer standing. The area is now employed as a city-owned parking lot.

This is the aftermath of the 1923 blizzard as seen on Rockland Road. This area of Rockland Road was once referred to as Rockaberry Hill. The house with the peak was located at 250 Rockland Road, near the top of Rockaberry Hill. The buildings as well as the hill disappeared when the arterial connecting the city centre with Somerset Street was built to provide a more direct route to the then newly built Regional Hospital in the early 1980s.

Three
AT THE FALLS

The high rocky cliffs at the Reversing Falls gorge provided the best location to anchor bridges spanning the St. John River at Saint John from 1853 onwards. That narrow space of about 600 feet was linked in the 19th century by two bridges, the 1853 Suspension Bridge and the 1885 Railway Bridge. In 1915, the new steel arched Reversing Falls Bridge would replace the wooden Suspension Bridge, and that is the point where we wish to continue the saga of the bridges.

As this picture indicates, the time for the Suspension Bridge was over and it was coming down in early 1916. Basically, the Suspension Bridge was a wooden platform that could not carry streetcars, as it was not electrified nor would it take the trolleys' weight. Further, it was only 23 feet wide with 15 feet for carriages in the centre and 4-foot sidewalks on each side.

The 1885 Railway Bridge had to be reinforced with two high steel trestles by 1915. In 1921 a new steel low trestle Railway Bridge was completed. The 1915 Reversing Falls Bridge and the 1921 Railway Bridge remain today on those high rocky cliffs where two to three bridges have spanned the heights since 1885.

Shortly before the 1853 Suspension Bridge (far right) was taken down in 1916 a total of three completely usable bridges were captured in this postcard. It was taken from the Provincial Hospital and shows a locomotive on the 1885 Railway Bridge (far left), which has two reinforced steel high trestles. Another feature is the work shack on the left side of the roadway leading into the bend of the new 1915 Reversing Falls Bridge (middle).

This postcard by the Valentine Company dates about 1918 when only two bridges crossed the Falls. The 1885 Railway Bridge (far left) has had the two high trestles airbrushed out while the near foreground track shows a number of supporting steel underpinning towers. The work shack is gone and eight vehicles are using the new bridge (1915), which has a nicely fenced sidewalk leading onto it at the bend. Only the abutments of the 1853 Suspension Bridge remain.

13

NEW C.P.R. BRIDGE, ST. JOHN, N.B.

Taken from the Cushing Sawmill, this postcard captures three bridges while we note that the 1915 Reversing Falls Bridge's steel arch construction can just barely be seen. On the new (1921) low-trestled Railway Bridge, a train is crossing over the eight granite block supports moving west towards Fairville. The old 1885 Railway Bridge, weakened and no longer usable, remains as the middle bridge. Its twin reinforced high trestles are back, and showing through those granite blocks are its steel supporting towers.

Approach to Bridges and Reversing Falls, Saint John, N. B. Canada.

This postcard shows our present two bridges. The 1921 Railway Bridge with a locomotive and the 1915 Reversing Falls Bridge were photographed from the knoll above the roadway across from Simms. The 1885 Railway Bridge is gone and only two granite towers mark its former placement between these two bridges. On the right hand side at the Falls sits the Trading Post, the forerunner to today's Reversing Falls Restaurant, while a passenger car and trolley proceed westerly towards Fairville.

TRADING POST
Reversing Falls, N.B.

The Trading Post was the first structure to formally serve the tourist trade at The Falls and this interior view shows a classy souvenir shop. Seated at the desk and doing a live remote broadcast is C.F.B.C.'s young Don Armstrong in the late 1940s era when radio was king. Don provided his local listeners with lively patter while interviewing tourists to The Falls and discussing where they were coming from. This was one of Don's earliest broadcasting assignments.

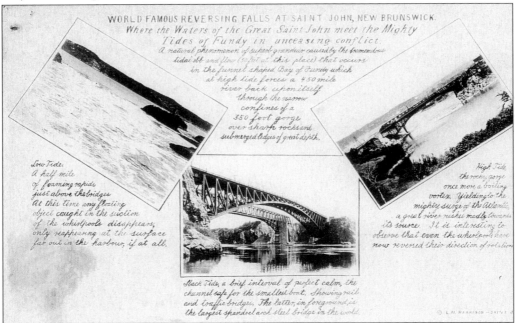

This real-photo postcard with three insets tries to show how the falls reverse while being spanned by our two present bridges. Tourists visiting the falls have extreme difficulty understanding the concept of a reversing falls. Even Saint Johners have great difficulty trying to explain the phenomenon to people from away. This card endeavours to explain the points of low, slack, and high tide at the falls.

Photographer Harold Climo's aerial shot of the bridges and the falls with the river running down at low tide gives an excellent portrayal of this natural phenomenon in the gorge. The Cushing Mill at Union Point above the falls is in full operation while twisted white water around the three islands shows the low tide effects just off Fallsview Park. This water is now impassable for all boats until the 20-minute slack tides (recent exceptions being the Jet Boat and kayakers).

This Climo photograph has captured the water power of the falls at low tide. From left to right, it starts at the two islands, Middle and Crow, and moves down under the bridges to Split Rock, where the white water whirlpools are surging. Above these two islands, to the right, a huge log raft fills Marble Cove. Two building complexes, the Ford Plant and the Provincial Hospital, are in the bottom left of the view on the western side of the bridges.

This panoramic shot, probably taken from the Douglas Avenue Meteorological Observatory, shows the upper river area above the falls that is just downriver from Indiantown. The focal point is the Murray & Gregory Ltd. lumber mill with the rafts of logs filling Marble Cove. The company was established in 1868 as a woodworking factory with its many buildings and its towering twin smokestacks. Regrettably, the downturn in the economy of the late 1980s sealed its demise in 1991.

This view of Union Point shows the Port Royal Pulp and Paper Mill on a property that has had a mill there for over 150 years. In this 1940s representation it is markedly different from the Cushing Mill of the turn of the century. Numerous fires over the years have changed the look of each new mill upon rebuilding. Today's Irving Pulp Mill continues to change its look yearly, adding scrubbers and other facilities designed to protect the environment.

Four

MISS CANADA AND OTHER CONTEMPORARIES

MISS CANADA, AND THE PRINCESS

During and after WW I, most celebrations and other special events in Saint John had been put on hold or at least scaled back and rather subdued. Even though the Allies had won the war, there was still a cloud of sorrow and lethargy hanging over the area with so many native sons losing their lives in the effort.

If there was any one event, which breathed life and energy back into the city, it would have to be the "Miss Canada" contest of 1923. It was a national event with all provinces represented. Here in Saint John, the winner of the "Times-Star Carnival Queen Contest" would automatically become "Miss St. John" and have a chance to compete in the "Miss Canada" contest to be held in Montreal. On the afternoon of January 27, 1923, at the Arena, Miss Winnifred Blair was chosen as the winner out of a field of 95 contestants. Two weeks later, after a week of competition, Miss Blair was chosen as Canada's fairest daughter and became the first "Miss Canada."

On this and the following pages, you will be introduced to Winnifred Blair as well as some other local citizens who achieved notoriety in the community. Our first view shows Miss Blair at Lily Lake with Beatrice McKinney, the Carnival Princess, on her right. This photograph was taken during the International Speedskating competition held in Saint John during the Winter Carnival.

Signed by Miss Canada, Winnifred C.I. Blair, are two postcard views of her in her official costume, taken at the studio of D. Smith Reid. The tailored skating outfit was made from jade cloth trimmed with white fur and a fur cap to match. The high skating boots sporting white fur tops were entirely silver in colour. Gold buttons completed the ensemble. The fur trimming for the costume was supplied by H. Mont Jones, while the tailoring was done by F. Guy MacKinnon.

In a real-photo card taken at the Climo Studio, we see Winnifred Blair in one of her casual skating outfits, which she took with her for her week-long stay in Montreal for the Miss Canada contest. This portrait was actually taken before she left. It can also be found bearing the title, "Miss St. John," and she was wearing the same outfit in a shot published in the papers after she won the Carnival Queen/Miss St. John contest.

This photograph was taken on February 12, 1923, during Miss Canada's arrival in St. John from Montreal. Here, the "Royal" coach which bore Miss Blair, Mrs. Walter Golding (chaperone), and Charles A. Owens (chairman of the reception committee) from Union Station to the Royal Hotel is seen amongst the thousands who were on hand to greet her. Notice the policemen beside and behind the coach, there to keep the multitude back. A few in the crowd turned to face the camera, including Miss Blair.

Here is a real-photo postcard of Miss Dorothy Oatey, who was selected as Miss St. John on February 16, 1924. As was the case in 1923, a group of judges made the selection at the Arena. Miss Oatey was chosen from a group of six finalists by a secret ballot, the results of which were not revealed until the following Monday afternoon, two days later. Miss Oatey was introduced to the public as Miss St. John at a hockey game that night between St. John and the "Abbies."

This shot shows the popular traffic policeman from the 1920s and 1930s, Andy Duffy. Shortly after joining the police force in May of 1920, he was assigned to direct traffic at the head of King. His amiable personality, cheerful attitude, attention to duty, and the way he went about his job with style and panache, all made him one of the most (if not the most) popular members ever to serve on the local police force.

Shown here is a studio portrait of Andy Duffy on a postcard published by the International Fine Art Co. Ltd., of Montreal. It shows Andy in a classic pose that he would have struck many times for tourists and locals alike, complete with his signature white gloves and his hat cocked to one side. This card would probably have been produced after November of 1923 when Andy won a 'most popular policeman' contest. In that contest he received a staggering 51,300 votes.

Andy Duffy, Popular Traffic Policeman, Saint John, N.B.

On December 25, 1923, our famous Mahaney quadruplets were born at home at 74 St. James Street. Proud parents Thomas and Lyda (Dresilla) Mahaney already had five children. Pictured here at three months, from left to right are: Edith May (3 pounds 4 ounces at birth), Edna Louise (3 pounds 8 ounces), Lyda Christine (5 pounds), and John Douglas, the only boy, weighed about 6 pounds. Dr. Stanley Bridges delivered them.

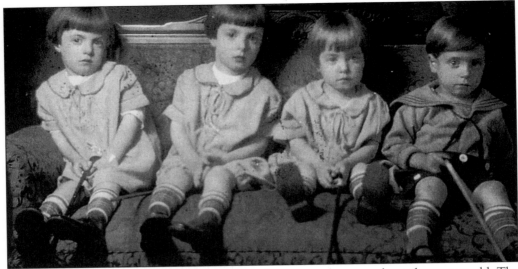

This second shot is a postcard of the quads, in the same order, now about three years old. The family was complete with two more children for a total of 11. Citizens of Saint John were very supportive of the Mahaneys, who often faced tough times financially. Just before Christmas of 1935, Archdeacon H.A. Cody, of St. James Anglican Church, announced assistance through a cheque from a Montreal couple. However, the parents never allowed the quads to become wards of the government.

Mahaney Quadruplets
at Eleven Years of age

This 1934 postcard showing the 11-year-old Mahaney quads marks a change in their degree of notoriety, as the Dionne quintuplets had been born that year. The Mahaneys led a very normal, happy, untroubled childhood. Between 1944 and 1947 all married, John Douglas (1923–1989) to Mildred Allen of Saint John, and the girls became Edna Louise Fairweather (1923–1996), while the two surviving quads, Edith May (McCully) McLaughlin and Lyda Christine Ryan are at present in their seventy-fifth year.

Five
THE BEATTY &
PANORAMAS

This chapter celebrates the great panoramas that were taken from the roof of the eight-story Admiral Beatty Hotel, which was completed in 1925. Located at the corner of King Square South and Charlotte Street, today, after its beautiful renovations, it continues to serve as a very functional Senior Citizens Complex.

In introducing this chapter we wish to begin at the end of an era with the Dufferin Hotel, whose four-story structure stood on the corner prior to the Admiral Beatty Hotel. Built in 1891, it is pictured here in 1924, when the Dufferin would soon be demolished. The large sign on the hotel offers building material for sale.

Stuart Trueman, writing in 1930 in the *Evening Times-Globe*, six years after the Dufferin Hotel's demolition, commented throughout the article on how building materials, antiques, and keepsakes were now on view in homes worldwide. In particular, film stars' homes in California were noted for having Dufferin artifacts on display. Further, due to the age of the wood and the straightness of its grain, the roof beams and room corner posts were used by violin makers. The Dufferin lives on through the fine violinists playing on former Dufferin building material.

This vertical postcard view shows the Admiral Beatty Hotel taken diagonally from Charlotte Street. The postcard highlights the cobblestone streets in front of the main King Square South and side Charlotte Street entrances. From its 1925 opening it became the city's pre-eminent hotel offering banquet and ballrooms for formal occasions. A number of business firms operated from this hotel location including C.H.S.J. Radio, which started its broadcasts from the hotel in 1934.

The Admiral Beatty Hotel was the 13-year project of S. Allan Thomas, senior member of Saint John's Thomas, Armstrong & Ball Investment Securities firm. Through steady hard work, his project was started in 1912 and resulted in the June 23, 1925 hotel opening. Thomas was successful after arranging the partnership of the United Hotels of America and the Admiral Beatty Hotel Co. that built the complex. Saint John citizens benefited from the $1.2 million hotel investment, of which $800,000 was new money brought into the city.

This is a view taken from the roof of the Admiral Beatty Hotel facing north, *c.* 1930. Some of the old hotels located along King Square North are seen here, including the Park, Edward, LaTour, and the Dunlop. The building on the corner of Charlotte and King Square North, once known as 'Breeze's Corner' (named after a long-standing 19th-century grocery owned by William and Dudne Breeze), was demolished in 1939 to make way for the Bank of Nova Scotia.

This is another view from the roof of the Beatty, facing northeast, *c.* 1934. It is a few years later than the previous view, showing the then recently completed Golden Ball building on the right. A close look will reveal several cars parked on the roof of the Golden Ball. Notice also one of the buildings from the previous view has been torn down and replaced by the tiny diner to the left of the Dunlop Hotel which was called 'Buckley's Quick Lunch.'

Here is an aerial view of the uptown area looking south. King Square is prominently featured with the Admiral Beatty and the Imperial Theatre on the far side in this 1929 photograph. On the left the old St. Malachi's Hall is visible, then being used by M & M Motors, Ltd., likely as a storage facility. To the right we see Trinity Church and adjacent to it the Masonic Temple, gutted by a fire which occurred on January 26, 1929.

This is another panorama taken from the roof of the Admiral Beatty, this time looking west in this c. 1945 view. The roof and steeple of the Trinity Church dominate the right side with St. Andrews farther to the left. The West Side docks are clearly visible in the background much as they appeared after the reconstruction of the 1930s.

Six
THE DRY DOCK

On Monday, October 29, 1923, the weather cleared up for the Opening Day Ceremonies of the Saint John Dry Dock and Shipbuilding Company in East Saint John. Mayor Fisher had declared a one-half day school holiday so that the children and teachers could attend the 3 p.m. afternoon opening and the parade to follow. Long awaited, this huge undertaking had been conceived in 1911 under Sir William Pugsley's efforts. He was able to persuade the Norton and Griffiths Company of London, England, to enter into the terms and conditions of construction of both a Dry Dock and Breakwater.

The company started building in 1912 and construction was well underway when the war started in 1914. Unfortunately, the circumstances of war shortages in men, materials, and money forced the Norton Griffiths firm into receivership in 1916. At that time work was suspended.

In 1918, the Saint John Dry Dock Company took up the task and completed the work, including the Courtenay Bay Breakwater of 7,700 feet and a dredged channel in Courtenay Bay.

Canada's governor general, Baron Byng of Vimy, arrived at noon by train, attended a luncheon at the Dry Dock for 350 guests, opened the Dry Dock, and quickly returned to Ottawa on the 4 p.m. train. The parade route was lined by thousands as the firemen, police, and Syrian Society won the prizes for floats. Another luncheon for guests was held at the Union Club and that night a ball at the Pythian Castle was hosted by the Dry Dock manager, Frank Ross.

This postcard shows the Dry Dock at its Courtenay Bay entrance. Its Fitting-Out Wharf is on the left side while the Lay-To Wharf is on the right. Straight ahead behind the caissoned opening lies the 1,150-feet Dry Dock, then the biggest in the world.

This real-photo postcard was taken from the Lay-To Wharf in 1923 and captures three men atop the floating gate. Across the Dry Dock from the left-hand edge, the Power House and the Machine Shop next to it look fully completed. Construction looks nearly finished on the top floor and the roof of the Plate, Boiler and Blacksmith Shops building, while the Joiner Shop seems ready for work.

This real-photo postcard shows the separating central caisson up in position while the inner dock of the Dry Dock fills. The close-up gives a good comparison of the size of the men at the top of the caisson to the flooding dock. Further, the shot focuses on the seldom seen, relatively undeveloped far side of the Dry Dock.

This fourth real-photo postcard of the 1923 new Dry Dock shows it in its completed state. There is a vessel being constructed in the Dock and the large cranes along its sides can be seen in this panorama looking towards Courtenay Bay with the central city peninsula in the background. This Dry Dock's yard used a marine railway docking system, which placed it ahead of contemporary dry docks.

Another shot taken in 1923 shows the central caisson separating the Dry Dock into two working docks. The vista of Courtenay Bay and a bit of the city can be seen in the distance. The moveable 20-ton travelling crane is operating on the ship in the outer dock. The left-hand side looks very incomplete and would remain so for some time.

This vertical postcard shows the working Dry Dock of a later time period. It was used as an advertisement for the Dry Dock stating on the back that, "The dock was capable of holding two ocean liners at the same time, being divided if need be, by a central caisson. Frequently when this dock is pumped out, the gateway is filled with wriggling fishes, the dock having acted as a weir that confined them in the area."

This later 1920s real-photo postcard shows two major ships being worked on with the central caisson down. In the foreground is the *Welland County* and behind sits the SS *Canadian Mariner*. The four men at the left-hand side seem to be overseeing the work. This dock was the first to solve the problem of the ship's waste disposal system, continuing to operate through a connecting delivery system that would be hooked up to the dock's own facilities.

The British Battle Cruiser, HMS *Norfolk* was in the Dry Dock in 1933 for repairs. The *Norfolk* in 1928 became the fourth British warship, dating from 1693, that carried that name. When completed in 1930, *Norfolk* carried a full complement of 650, was 630 feet in length, 66 feet in the beam, with a 17-foot draught. The 10-ton *Norfolk* survived the Second World War giving meritorious service.

The aerial view on this postcard shows an extremely busy Dry Dock site at the end of World War II. Four ships are occupying the two bays of the main facility. Another ship can be seen in the parallel Auxillary Tidal Dock. Five ships are tied up at the outside wharves of the main Dry Dock's entrance. Farther into Courtenay Bay vessels are tied up at both the International Fertilizer plant and the Irving Oil tank farm.

This photograph shows the launching of the Canadian Navy Corvette, *Amherst*, on December 4, 1940. *Amherst* was the first of three (*Sackville* and *Moncton* were the others) to be built at the Saint John Dry Dock during the Second World War. *Amherst* was commissioned on August 5, 1941, and provided meritorious service throughout the war. On July 16, 1945, *Amherst* was paid off.

Canada's Naval Aircraft Carrier, the *Magnificent*, was under refit from mid-June to mid-October 1949 at the Dry Dock. Affectionately known as "The Maggie," she had been started in 1944, but was not completed by war's end. Commissioned on April 7, 1948, "The Maggie" went on to play a key role in Canada's peace-keeping effort during the 1956 Suez Canal Crisis. In 1957, H.M.C.S. Bonaventure took on the *Magnificent's* role, and she was paid off on April 10, 1957.

Seven

SHIPPING

On February 4, 1919, at 2 p.m., thousands crowded the shores near the Reversible Falls to witness the launching of the four-masted steam schooner, *Randfontein*. Built by D.H. Sakar of the Marine Construction Company, her keel was laid immediately following the launching of the ill-fated Schooner *Dornfontein*, on June 11, 1918. The *Dornfontein* was twice a victim of fire. Stopped on her maiden voyage by the German U-Boat #56 and set afire, she was salvaged, reconstructed, and renamed the *Netherton* by the firm of Pushee Brothers, of Dennyville, Maine, only to be abandoned on fire in mid-ocean in August 1920. The *Randfontein* and *Dornfontein* were the only vessels ever launched sideways in Saint John, but they were not sister ships, despite the similarity in naming. The *Randfontein* was much larger, being 230 feet long with a beam of 38 feet and a gross weight of about 1,200 tons, while the Dornfontein was 186 by 40 feet weighing 695 tons.

The launching of these two vessels, along with the *War Fundy* and *War Moncton*, from a Marsh Creek yard marked the end of a brief revival of what had been a great tradition in Saint John, the building and sailing of ocean-going wooden ships. Many traditional aspects of shipping in Saint John have been lost over the years. Harbour ferries were a fixture in the city until the early 1950s when the service was discontinued. Passenger ships were once regular visitors to Saint John. Better roads and the emergence of commercial airlines brought this form of travel to an end, not only in this city, but also in much of the world. The loading and unloading of ships was for years done by fairly equal portions of man and machine. That too has changed drastically by such advents as containers and roll-on/roll-off vessels.

Still, in spite of all the changes, some traditions endure. Ferry services between Saint John (Millidgeville) and the Kingston Peninsula, as well as between Saint John and Digby, N.S., continue today as reminders of our past.

This photograph shows the wooden steamer, *War Fundy*, which was launched on Saturday, August 4, 1918, from the Grant & Horne Shipyard in Courtenay Bay. Built for the British Admiralty, hers was the first launch in Courtenay Bay in 30 years. The 250-foot vessel at 2,800 tons was constructed of native yellow birch and Bay Shore spruce for framing and planking the craft. Mrs. Carvell, wife of Canada's minister of public works, christened the ship as she slid into her namesake Fundy tide.

This picture shows Reed's Point about 1910 when it was the prime docking facility on the east side of the harbour. The Eastern Steamship Company Terminal operated the Boston boats and the C.P.R.'s Digby to Saint John *Princess Helene* docked just above here from the 1930s to the early 1950s. At that time, the expanded Pugsley Terminal was constructed to replace the old wooden wharves.

In March of 1931, the International Fertilizer Co., Ltd. was completed. Built on man-made land from a side hill at the Dry Dock, it was located between the Dock and Irving Oil. This one-story wooden building, the largest of its type in the Maritimes, was 450 feet long, 250 feet wide, and 33 feet high. This December 1931 photograph shows the SS *Torrhead* unloading a cargo of bulk fertilizer raw material for manufacture. The company closed in 1968.

The United Fruit Company sent their ships laden with tons of bananas through the port of Saint John in the late 1920s. A very labour intensive situation transferred the cargo from ship to Canadian Pacific Railway special ice-cars. The bananas were then shipped to major Eastern Canadian markets. The trade gradually declined by the early 1950s but West Side residents fondly remember the "Banana Boat's" arrival and their resulting banana splits.

The *Empress* was built in 1906 and arrived on the Saint John to Digby, Bay of Fundy C.P.R. Service in 1916. The *Empress* replaced the *Yarmouth* on that run but she was not designed for the rapidly expanding automobile age. Her crew often had great difficulties with freight handling, which involved teams of horses hauling or dragging cargo to and from the cargo holds. The *Empress* was laid up in Saint John in 1930 when the *Princess Helene* arrived.

This photograph shows the *Empress* on the rocky ledge at Black Point near Mispec at the outer perimeter of the harbour. In April of 1922, she was making her way back to Saint John from Digby in the fog when the currents drove her onto the rocks. The *Empress* was lightened and at a higher tide pulled off the rocks by tugs. The June 22, 1931 West Side Docks fire gutted the *Empress* and she spent her remaining days as a C.P.R. harbour coal barge.

The *Princess Helene* was built specifically for the Bay of Fundy service at Dunbarton on the Clyde River, Scotland. Arriving in 1930 to replace the *Empress,* the *Princess Helene* could carry five hundred passengers and 50 automobiles. The *Princess Helene* was the real workhorse of this run, and after 33 years in 1963 she was sold. Her new Greek owners fitted her out as a cruise ship in the Mediterranean Sea. She was renamed the *Carina II* and in this easier role she served well into the 1970s.

The SS *Saint John,* the last of the 'Boston' boats, was launched at Newport, Virginia on January 9, 1932, with a bottle of water from Reversing Falls. She was purchased by the U.S. Navy in 1941 for $2,782,500. Renamed the *Antaeus,* she saw service as a submarine tender and a troop transport before ending up as a hospital ship called the *Rescue.* She earned battle stars at Okinawa and the home islands of Japan. Retired from service, she was scrapped in 1958.

The Millidgeville ferry has served that community and residents of the Kingston Peninsula since the 1800s. In 1892, the first "Maggie Miller" started her run for about 40 years as a well-beloved side-wheeler. She charged fares of 10¢ for passengers and 20¢ for horse teams and their teamster. In 1934, the Maggie Miller II replaced the first vessel under substantial funding by the Province of New Brunswick. Eventually, fares were dropped because the Provincial Department of Highways made ferries part of their toll-free road system.

Steam-operated ferry boats, like the *Governor Carleton* above, shuttled passengers on the harbour's City—West Side route from 1838. The boats of our century were, in order: the *Ouangondy* (Indian word for Navy Island), 1870–1908; Western Extension, 1870s–1910; the *Ludlow*, 1905–1933; the *Governor Carleton* (launched in Rhode Island as the Newport in 1907) 1911–1933; and lastly, the screw propellered Loyalist, 1933–1953.

Eight
SPEEDSKATING

Before the rise of hockey, basketball, or any of the more popular winter sports of the present, speedskating was one of the biggest winter sporting attractions in Canada and much of the United States and Europe from the 1880s to the 1930s. In Saint John, speedskating was probably the most popular sport of all during those years.

Beginning in the 1880s with the emergence of Hugh McCormick, through to Charlie Gorman and Willie Logan in the 1920s and 1930s, Saint John developed a reputation for world-class speedskaters. Gorman began racing in 1907 and went on to win the Maritime Senior Championship in 1912. He served overseas in WW I where he fought in such famous battles as Vimy Ridge and Hill 70, and, after being wounded in the right leg in September of 1918, he was sent home. After the war, having recuperated from his wounds, Gorman began skating again. He returned to top form in 1921 and although there would be disappointments from time to time, he reached his peak in 1926 when he won the World Amateur Championship at Lily Lake.

Our first view shows Willie Logan (left) and Gorman (right) with Miss Canada (Winnifred Blair) in the middle, their images superimposed on a shot of the ice structure erected at King Square for the International Skating Championships in 1923.

Above is a real-photo postcard view of the Canadian Amateur Speedskating Championships which took place at Lily Lake on January 18–19, 1922. Between ten and fifteen thousand spectators were on hand for the races hoping to see Charlie Gorman win, but his performance was perhaps the worst of his career as he failed to score any points at the meet.

This is a photograph of "Human Dynamo," Charlie Gorman. Gorman was a brash, outgoing, confident man whose ability and determination not only made him into a world champion speedskater, but also a sports idol whose popularity in Saint John remains unequalled. On February 24, 1927, school was cancelled and businesses closed as countless thousands showed up at the Victoria Hotel to welcome back Gorman who had just defended his world title.

Pictured above is a portion of the huge grandstand built especially for the 1926 World Amateur Speedskating Championships that took place from January 26 to 28. Crowds in excess of 50,000 people attended the three-day meet. Rush seats sold for 50¢ apiece, a tidy sum in 1926. Official programs were issued each day that sold for 10¢ each.

In this view the Union Jack floats in the breeze shortly after having been hoisted by Lieutenant-Governor Todd, and the Stars and Stripes are being run up by Romeyn Wormuth, United States Consul. The photograph was taken during the flag-raising ceremony with which the world's championship skating meet opened at Lily Lake on January 26, 1926.

"On your mark, get set, go!" The photographer captures the start of two of the many races held at the 1926 World Championships. A portion of the pavilion and the huge crowd of spectators in attendance can be seen in the background. Notice the hardy souls to the right of the pavilion who climbed atop a pole to get a bird's-eye view of the race.

This is a sprint to the wire, or in this case to the string. The camera captures a close finish of one of the races from 1926. The finish line was a string stretched across the track tied to broom handles held on either side by a track official, one of which is seen here on the right. Notice the loose string hanging from his coat, no doubt pre-cut lengths to be used as needed.

A number of times during the three-day meet in 1926 spectators were entertained between races by a variety of "fancy acts." Among them were Norval Baptie and Gladys Lamb, the "World's Premier Fancy Skating team," direct from Madison Square Garden. Another popular event was barrel jumping, shown in this view. The barrels were supplied by the Provincial Lime Co. Ltd., located at Brookville where Brookville Manufacturing continues in business today.

Wm. Logan

Here is Willie Logan in a classic pose at Lily Lake. In 1926 he was the young heir apparent to Charlie Gorman. Logan, competing with the Seniors for the first time, finished second on three occasions, including the 5-mile final won by Charlie Gorman. He would go on to distinguish himself, and amongst his accomplishments were two bronze medals at the 1932 Olympics which made him the first New Brunswick athlete ever to win an Olympic medal.

E. d Snodgrass

Ed Snodgrass was a contemporary of Willie Logan. Both were 19 at the 1926 meet, and although Snodgrass wasn't as successful as Logan he still placed well in preliminary heats and made most of the finals. His performance earned him a spot on the Senior circuit that toured the major tracks in Canada and the United States.

At the International Championship meet held at Lily Lake in 1923, Saint Johners were looking for Charlie Gorman to claim the title. Nagging injuries held Gorman back and he finished a disappointing fifth. Shown here is Charles Jewtraw, a speedy, consistent skater from Lake Placid, New York, who went on to win the championship. During the meet, Jewtraw set a new world's outdoor record in the 220-yard event with a time of 18 4/5 seconds.

Here is Gladys Robinson of Toronto at the 1923 Championships. Miss Robinson claimed the Senior Ladies' title, dominating her division by winning all four events. Rose Johnson of Chicago finished second in all four finals. Although she pushed the winner a couple of times, Gladys Robinson was clearly the class of the field.

Gorman & Thunberg

Here are Charlie Gorman and Clas Thunberg after a workout at Lily Lake a few days before the 1926 Championships. Clas Thunberg, from Finland, was an Olympic gold medalist in 1924 and was the favorite to win at Saint John. However, Thunberg was unable to handle the North American style of racing and only managed one third place finish in the seven finals. He was very gracious in defeat and was a fan favorite throughout.

Pictured above are the front row box seats at the 1926 Championships at Lily Lake. The huge grandstands, built on either side of the pavilion, were jam-packed. This picture is likely from the third day of the meet, as the weather featured snow and high winds, and the evidence is all over the spectators. It failed to dampen their spirits, however, as they all appear to be enjoying themselves to the fullest.

Nine

THE WEST SIDE DOCKS

The West Side docks underwent a massive construction period in the late 1920s at the time that the Saint John Harbour Commission took over the harbour facilities from the city. This transformed a residential area that ran down in very close vicinity to the docks. The mill pond, located behind the docks in the middle of the residential area between Rodney and St. John Streets in one direction and between Ludlow and Union Streets in the other, would be completely filled in when construction stopped in the mid-1930s. The world's largest cofferdam was erected so that new, first-rate docks could be built to handle large vessels.

Navy Island was the key puzzle piece in the building of the cofferdam that forever closed off Buttermilk Channel, between Navy Island and Carleton Point, from the Bay of Fundy tides at the mouth of the St. John River. The cofferdam successfully permitted new pier construction until completion in 1934. It was only breached once, in February of 1930, in all its time of holding back the great tidal surges.

In the middle of construction, the Great Port Fire swept through, destroying the existing piers 8 through 14 on June 22, 1931. The Harbour Commission was able, by having construction crews working 24 hours a day using floodlights, to have the winterport ready for the 1931–32 season. The fire, in a fortunate side effect, offered many West Siders employment in creating the new dock facilities at the beginning of the Great Depression.

The photograph above opens the chapter with a view from Blue Rock, overlooking Queen Street and the Mill Pond taken in the early 1920s. The buildings visible at the port facility would be lost to the Port Fire in 1931.

This early photograph, c. 1915, focuses on the six berths off Sand Point Slip. Five ships are tied up and only one spot is vacant. The ship at the far left is at berth #1. The ship in the centre of the photograph is at berth #3. Directly across the slip on the right-hand side is a ship at berth #6. The other two ships have only their masts showing.

On June 13, 1917, the collapse of No. 5 shed occurred at the West Side docks. No lives were lost only because the collapse took place a few minutes past noon. Three gangs of C.P.R. workers had just left for their lunch and the few who remained were close enough to an open door to make a narrow escape.

This aerial photograph shows the whole area that the Saint John Harbour Commission acquired in 1927. The *Frederick Elkin*, one of the last four-masted schooners, is entering the harbour. The lower West Side neighborhood properties would be expropriated below Marketplace. The millpond was filled in with spoilage from inside the excavated cofferdam. A railway freight yard was then built over the lower half of the former millpond and what had been lower West Side properties.

One of the first new port facilities to be completed was this Harbour Board grain elevator pictured in nearly completed state in 1930. To the immediate right of the structure the clock tower of Union Street's post office is prominent. The grain elevator escaped the 1931 Fire, as the prevailing winds were to its south where the fire started. About 1990, this largely cement structure was demolished as grain shipments no longer used Saint John by the late 1980s.

This 1930 view captures the West Side docks in pre-fire vintage with the cofferdam in its early stages of construction. The upper and lower connecting wings of the dam are meeting Navy Island and blocking Buttermilk Channel's passage. The new grain elevator stands out in white cement at the inside edge of the dam's basin. The homes on Union Street and up towards Marketplace have been thinned out by expropriation.

This c. 1930 photograph shows the method of movement of spoilage from the cofferdam site. The train of wooden hopper cars would be filled with the excavated material from inside the cofferdam. The hopper cars were then hauled across to the millpond where their spoilage was dumped in to fill it. Half of the filled-in millpond became Harbour Commission property below Marketplace. Above Marketplace to Ludlow Street the filled-in millpond became the City's property.

Pictured is the West Side docks ablaze on June 22, 1931, as seen from the hills of Fort Howe. The fire consumed most of the existing docks and supporting facilities with the new Navy Island docks still under construction. Today, virtually everything in this photograph is either gone or altered to such an extent that it would be unrecognizable to the photographer.

This view is of the 1931 West Side dock fire from Strait Shore. The newly constructed grain elevator, prominent in this view, was spared from the flames. Just below it is the Marine Dock, complete with a sizable shed which has long since disappeared. To the left were a few remaining residential buildings located on Middle Street, which was swallowed up by the port expansion.

These were the newly completed c. 1936 Navy Island facilities. Prominent in the view are sheds A and B, later sheds #2 and #3, showing their grain conveyers and rail lines that serviced them. Navy Island proper, other than providing an excellent landsite that allowed for easier construction of the cofferdam, had few functional uses. For years, until the Harbour Bridge ramp was built over it, that former Navy Island land lay idle. Now it serves as an excellent storage area.

This aerial view from the early 1940s shows the West Side docks and much of the lower West Side. The millpond is filled in and much of the new rail yard has been completed, built mostly on the expropriated land between Market Place and Union Street. The new docks on the left and the rebuilt docks on the right are a stark contrast to what the area looked like before the 1930s.

Ten

STATIONS, VIADUCTS,
AND THE HARBOUR BRIDGE

The Union Depot shown in this side view, capturing the hillside in front of Rockland Road, was built in 1884. Early station agents occupied the upper floor as their residence, but by the late 1920s various groups would rent out the rooms on the second and third floors. In 1918, the Depot became Union Station when, under the Canadian Government's direction, the Canadian National and Canadian Pacific Railways became partners.

The C.N.R. was the Depot's owner through a historic inheritance, from the original 1853 station in Saint John. This chapter will attempt to show linkage between the two Union Stations, the two Mill Street Viaducts eventually built, and the new Harbour Bridge that, when completed, covers a period of more than 40 years.

In 1927, the Saint John Harbour Commission took over management of the harbour, the docks, and the ferries. The 1928 proposal of a new Harbour Bridge would eliminate the ferry terminal and provide the Harbour Commission with new land acquisition. Mayor White and his Council by 1930 were fully behind the 1928 proposed Harbour Bridge route.

September of 1930 brought Sir Henry Thornton, C.N.R. president, to Saint John, where he announced a new station was to be built almost immediately. Further, Sir Henry wanted the traffic problems of the Mill Street crossing eliminated through the construction of a viaduct. Lastly, Sir Henry posed questions about the new Harbour Bridge proposal in relation to a new viaduct in the bridge's proposed Mill Street ramp.

This photograph shows the traditional railway valley with the new train sheds built in 1928 behind the old Depot. These new train sheds helped the C.N.R. make the decision in 1930 to demolish the old Depot. The picture is somewhat later than 1930 as the new Saint John General Hospital of 1931 can be seen completed on its Hospital Hill site in beige brick.

This frontal photograph of the old Depot, showing its minaret on the left side, also shows a teamster driving his horse and wagon over the Mill Street crossing. Mayor White and his Council agreed with Sir Henry's point about the viaduct and wanted movement on both the viaduct problem and the proposed Harbour Bridge. Joint action with the C.N.R. was suggested in meetings with railway commissioners in late 1930 after the old Depot had already been demolished.

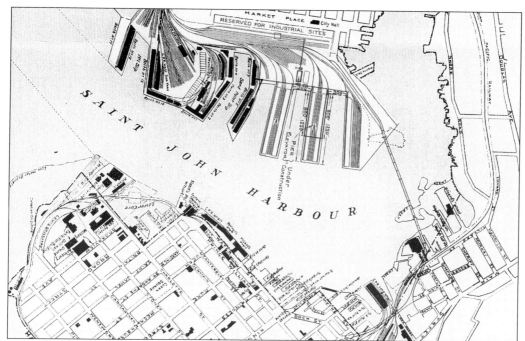

This map in the 1928 Harbour Commission Report represents the proposed route of the Harbour Bridge. It was felt by the city fathers and the Harbour Commission that the C.N.R. was a player in lobbying for a bridge with rail connections to the West Side. However, by 1932, with the completion of the new Union Station, it seemed that C.N.R. and C.P.R. had worked out arrangements to their own satisfaction for use of the C.P.R. Reversing Falls Railway Bridge.

This photograph shows the new Union Station that was quietly opened at 6 a.m., March 8, 1933 by J.M. Thompson, the terminal superintendent. He simply unlocked the impressively columned Pond Street main entrance, then, without fanfare beckoned Miss Mary Briggs, daughter of C.N. shed foreman Herbert Briggs, to be the first to enter. Both main and side entrances, on Pond and Mill Streets, had large electronic clocks. At this time the viaduct and the level crossing problems had not been solved.

This photograph shows the Mill Street traffic existing at this time when looking towards the level crossing in front of the new Union Station from Union Street. Agreement was finally reached which delayed the viaduct, but improved the traffic situation at the crossing. C.N.R. was given a right of way and in return the City leased some of their land for 20 years to allow for a widened Mill Street from Pond Street to Main Street over the level crossing.

This photograph shows the beautiful interior of the new Union Station. The full two-story height was used in creating the spacious waiting room area. The ticket office was located at the eastern business end of the concourse. Across the wide waiting area was Susie Murphy's Restaurant, a soda fountain, and News Stand. Through the eastern end of the concourse, doors led out to the lobby where access to the tracks and baggage and parcel checking rooms could be gained.

This photograph moves the time 18 years ahead to the new Mill Street Viaduct's baby carriage ramp that is under construction in August 1951. The view, looking south, profiles Union Station on its track side with the city in the background. The connection has been made between the nearly completed viaduct and the station at the first story level walkway. Directly above Union Station, in the distance, we see the old YMCA building that is undergoing demolition.

An exterior view of Union Station also shows its newly constructed Mill Street Viaduct connection in November 1951. This construction, which solved the traffic problem, had been delayed nearly 20 years. The proposed Harbour Bridge project would remain shelved for almost another 14 years. The Mill Street Viaduct connected from both roadsides with Union Station by stairwells that descended one story level. A later viaduct, in 1969, would be required construction for the Harbour Bridge/Throughway link.

This aerial shot shows the 1951 completed Viaduct. The ramps as set up would be fine for 18 years until a connection with the new Harbour Bridge's off-ramp at the Red Rose Tea Building would become necessary. On the far side of Union Station, the Mill Street Viaduct's off-ramp would connect with the westbound Harbour Bridge/Throughway traffic. By the end of November 1973, the C.N.R. had announced Union Station was to be demolished.

Saint Johners mourned the fact that C.N.R. did not leave Union Station intact, as it was fondly remembered, to serve for large civic functions. This May 1970 photograph shows the newly completed four-lane Harbour Bridge. The Canadian government built the Harbour Bridge creating New Brunswick's only Toll Bridge whose principal building debt seems unlikely to be paid off. The Saint John passenger railway link is gone now, only a memory of the past.

Eleven
MILLIDGEVILLE AIRPORT

From 1929 until our present airport opened in 1951, Millidgeville Airport was the city's prime landing site for airlines. Located close to the junction of Boar's Head Road and Millidge Avenue, the runway's southern end started across from today's Millidgeville Fire Station on Millidge Avenue and ran north down what is today Donaldson Street.

During the initial years, the airport was a stopping off place for fliers who were on their way to Newfoundland. From there, the fliers would attempt Trans-Atlantic flights. Amelia Earhart, the famous female flier of the 1930s, stopped off at this airport on May 19 and 20, 1932, before going on to complete her ground-breaking solo flight of the Atlantic Ocean.

Built on a swamp, surrounded by hills and slopes, the airport was filled in with crushed rock with runways left unpaved. By 1938, the city realized its mistake and was about to pave the runways. The war years brought new facilities for the airport built by the R.C.A.F.; they were used for stationing their planes as pilots made forays over the Bay of Fundy. Later, after closing, many Saint Johners received their first driving skills practicing on the old airport runways.

This interesting photograph of Germany's new Hindenburg Zeppelin was taken on Millidge Avenue about where the Irving Convenience Store is located today. A tractor grader is grading Millidge Avenue while the lighter-than-air craft hovers above the city in the distance on this June 24, 1936. Many Saint Johners snapped photos of this foreign craft at various locations around the city. It moved quickly across the city at noon that day, hovering over the harbour and drydock, before heading off for Germany.

Here is another shot of the famous German zeppelin, "Hindenburg," near the completion of her unannounced visit, passing over a very rural-looking East Saint John. After receiving word that the ship was heading towards the city, CHSJ radio began advising the public of her impending arrival. There was a mad dash for cameras, and many photographers, amateur and professional, were able to catch the huge airship on film. Among her passengers that day was the famous German boxer, Max Schmelling.

Here, arriving from Boston at 4:45 p.m., August 1, 1931, is the inaugural flight of Pan American Airways Inc., a passenger and mail service. Using the world's largest Sikorsky amphibian, S-41, and starting at Boston, it made stops at Portland, Bangor, Calais, Saint John, and finally Halifax. It could fly from Boston to Saint John in three hours and ten minutes. Aboard this flight was city editor C.W. Gilchrist, of the *Evening Times Globe*, who would write his impressions of the trip for Saint John readers.

Pan American maintained an office at the municipal airport in Millidgeville with C.D. Wright, their resident representative of this "Maritime Air Limited" service. The plane carried 15 passengers, including a crew of three. Mail could not be carried if originating in Saint John for Halifax nor could it originate from Halifax for Saint John because it was being operated by a non-Canadian company. Laws prohibited non-Canadian companies engaging in any commercial activities between points in Canada.

Air mail rates of 6¢ for the first ounce and 10¢ for additional ounces prevailed in 1931. A registered letter required an extra 10¢. The city's Millidgeville municipal airport and sea base looks very rustic in these three photos with its gravel runways. Bill Giggey, lifelong Millidgeville resident, relates, "My older brother and I provided security for Pan Am on their initial flight requiring an overnight stay. As teenagers we slept that night in the Sikorsky Amphibian."

Maritime Central Airways maintained a small office at the sea base just above their hangar and dock (near top left corner). This photograph taken during the spring freshet in Brothers Cove also shows Grenville Ring's houseboat. Grenville, a well-known boatbuilder, is in the picture at the outboard motor with two curious unidentified children. The sea base, located just off Manners Sutton Road and Millidge Avenue, was a very busy spot at times, especially during WW II.

The Westland Lysander, Army co-operation plane, was also known as "Lizzie." It was a slow, high-winged monoplane, best for short takeoffs and landings. The plane was very lightly armed and would have a pilot and a gunner. Its support role was in reconnaissance or covert operations. Built in England, these planes could fly spies in behind the enemy lines in France. Definitely not a battle plane, Lysanders were also built in Toronto, Canada.

This is a photograph of the 71 men in the Royal Canadian Air Force 118th Squadron in front of their #423 Lysander. The picture was taken about 1941 at the Millidgeville Airport's R.C.A.F. component where this group would have been responsible to Eastern Air Command. These men made flights in Lysanders over the Bay of Fundy looking for enemy vessels. They also practiced dropping bombs and towing drogues for anti-aircraft gunners' target practice while stationed on Partridge Island.

This photograph of the Millidgeville Airport was taken just after the Second World War. The Maritimes Central Airways office is to the right of the hangar and their Beechcraft plane is taxied up in front. It would be delivering mail in the contract it had for the cities of Charlottetown, Summerside, Moncton, and Saint John. It could carry up to four passengers along with mail cargo for the government of Canada.

This photograph shows a weatherman, Art Gould, and his wife Lillian at the Millidgeville Airport standing in front of a C.F.D.P.I. Fleet Canuck. These planes were used by the Sturgeon Air Services, which was based in Fredericton. Primarily, they were used for private flying instruction lessons to the general public. Both before and after the war the airport had flying clubs available for Saint Johners.

In December 1952, Irving Oil pilot Jimmy Wade and his lone passenger, K.C. Irving, had just taken off when their C.F.G.P.A. Grummand Mallard crashed. Art Gould, then meteorologist at the Millidgeville airport, was one of the first to arrive on the scene and snapped this photograph. Both Mr. Wade and Mr. Irving scrambled safely out of the wreckage. Mr. Irving, in his unflappable manner intoned, "Mr. Gould, you can cancel our flight plan, we won't be going anywhere today."

Twelve
CHURCHES AND SCHOOLS

Portland Methodist Church was built on Portland Street in the City of Portland in 1826. This ground was given by the Hon. Charles Simonds, speaker of the Province's House of Assembly, and afforded a commanding view of the harbour. Long before the City of Portland would amalgamate with Saint John in 1889 three churches would occupy this site. The first two churches were destroyed by fire in 1841 and 1877 while the third, built in 1878, would serve as a landmark for over 90 years.

On June 14, 1970, the final service was held in the old Portland Church. The City's North End Urban Renewal in the area was to claim, by demolition, the 92-year-old structure. For 144 years the site had served as a church, and 47 ministers had preached the Word, 1826–1970.

The congregation had decided upon a new 14-acre site, and on September 27, 1970 the official opening and dedication of the new Portland United Church took place. It is located just off Millidge Avenue at Newport Crescent in the old North End where it continues its services today.

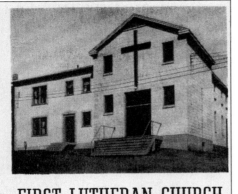

FIRST LUTHERAN CHURCH

4 SECOND STREET, SAINT JOHN, N. B.
(Off Cranston Ave., 2 blocks from Rockland Rd.)

PHONE 693-1063

WORSHIP 11:00 A.M., SUNDAY

REV. ERNEST A. FELKER, Pastor

Remember the Sabbath Day to Keep it Holy.
Exodus 20:8

The Hope Lutheran Church's community roots began in 1931 when the Elijah Danish Lutheran Church fulfilled a need by serving the many Danish immigrants who had arrived in Saint John during the 1920s. Their first location was on Rockland Road, but eventually, the congregation acquired the former Millidge family home at 4 Second Street in 1936. Fire in March 1949 destroyed that structure and in August 1950, on the original foundation, today's church as pictured here was dedicated.

St. Mary's Anglican Church was located at 207–211 Waterloo Street just below the General Public Hospital of the early 1860s. In 1930 the new General was dominant on the hill above the church and gradually, with its new wings, encroached on St. Mary's property. In 1967 the old church was torn down and a parking space was created for the General's increasing demands. The majority of St. Mary's congregation joined St. Paul's Anglican Valley Church.

St. Clement's Anglican Church was built in 1901 to serve the Millidgeville community, and it did so until 1969. The home in this 1930 photograph that was almost directly across the road was the Brayley house. Today, the old church building serves as the private residence of carver Gerald Oram, at 28 Manners Sutton Road. St. Clement's Church continues on in a new church that was built off Millidge and Daniel Avenues, in a shared structure with the Mission Church, in 1970.

Victoria Street Baptist Temple

Cor. Victoria and Durham Streets

ST. JOHN, N. B.

REV. G. D. HUDSON, B.TH.

𝕿his 𝕮ertifies that

the Bearer has purchased

BRICKS in the New Victoria Street Temple

✠

Building Commenced July 26, 1920.   To be Completed early in 1921.   Estimated Cost, $75,000.
Laying of Cornerstone, October 2, 1920.

The Victoria Street Baptist Church used this sketched certificate card to show that the owner had contributed financially to their building fund. The congregation of the church met all their proposed goals and an even more impressive building was completed in 1921. Unfortunately, by 1972, this structure had deteriorated beyond their financial means. The congregation joined with Main Street Baptist Church, just two blocks away, and in 1973 the church at the corner of Victoria and Durham Streets was demolished.

St. George's Church was completed in 1821 and is Saint John's oldest church. This wooden structure has undergone many changes over that time and the representation used is closer to today's structure. Located on the city's West Side this was the Anglican Church for the Parish of Carleton on Watson Street occupying the block between King and Duke Streets. Saint John's first mayor, Gabriel Ludlow, living on the West Side, purchased his pew in 1805 but died before the structure was completed.

New Albert School, completed in 1922 on Duke Street West, was an addition to adjacent Watson Street's Old Albert School built in 1876. Old Albert burned six years later in 1928. The West Side's beloved New Albert was especially known for its high standards that prepared students for life very successfully. New Albert faces King Square West's Courtney Hill that traditionally was the boys' school playgrounds. Sadly, due to financial considerations, New Albert was closed by the Provincial Department of Education in 1997.

This photograph shows a young Bobby Ring, armed and ready, in front of the Millidgeville school on Manners Sutton Road. It was located just above the seaplane base in this early 1940s shot. Traditionally, a schoolhouse had existed on this street from 1878, when a 50 by 100-foot lot was leased from R.V. DeBury at 25¢ per annum. It cost $900 to build, and later, when the union of Saint John and Portland occurred in 1889, a further $240 was spent for repairs and painting.

In 1926, the Saint John Vocational School opened with an enrollment of 401. The director, Fletcher Peacock, was to be at the helm of the Douglas Avenue structure until 1937. Mr. Peacock reported an increase to 597 students for the 1929–30 school year. That enrollment consisted of 216 junior high school students, 93 in industrial, 52 in home economics, 19 in commercial art, 51 in technical high school, and 166 in the commercial course. Moving with the times, the school name was changed to Harbour View High in 1997.

St. Vincent's High School, shown here under construction in 1917, opened in 1919 on Cliff Street. It was built for girls being taught next door at St. Vincent's Convent. As fate would have it, the boys had to use this new building because their school on Sydney Street could no longer house them. It existed as all boys until they moved to their new St. Malachy's High School in 1954. The girls then moved into St. Vincent's and it remains an all-girls school today.

On March 23, 1931, work began on the new Saint John High School at 170–200 Prince William Street opposite the Customs House. Opening for classes on September 6, 1932, it replaced the old Union Street Saint John High School that became a junior high until it closed in 1957. This new structure was built on a post-1877 Great Fire vacant lot. This postcard presentation of the 1935 graduation class may be seen with other framed photographs on the building's hallway walls.

Thirteen

HOSPITALS AND
LANDMARKS

A number of hospitals that fell beyond our time frame in our first book, 1900–1915, are being covered in this chapter. These were the buildings that cared for our beloved ones at crucial times in their lives. The Saint John General Hospital's recent demolition in December 1995, when it was imploded, has especially rekindled fond memories.

The first new hospital was the Saint john Tuberculosis Hospital built in 1915 on the East Side off the Red Head Road (now Bayside Drive). On the West Side, the School for the Deaf at the former Jewett estate was turned into a military hospital complex in 1918. Lastly, our beloved Saint John General Hospital opened in 1931, replacing the old General Public Hospital of the early 1860s, is at the same location at the upper end of Hospital Street.

The first photograph shows Saint John's "General Public Hospital" which opened in 1863 and continued to serve our citizens for 67 years until it closed in 1930. Sitting on what often is called Hospital Hill today, it was a three-story building with a basement foundation. The structure had eastern and western wings that ran off a central administrative wing that had connecting passages.

Looking east c. 1890, probably from the cupola of the Hazen house, the right side of the photograph shows the General Public Hospital in profile. In the central administrative core a tall cupola rises a further story and is topped with a jaunty hat-like structural design.

This photograph shows the General Public Hospital under demolition on April 24, 1930. Its eastern wings are completely gone and the upper part of the administrative core and its cupola have been demolished. The front western wing has been clearly demolished and its connecting passage to the administrative core has been exposed. Its rear counterpart still stands awaiting obliteration. The work cart, just off the front left corner sidewalk, displays a large sign, warning: DANGEROUS.

This real-photo postcard shows a newly completed "Saint John General Hospital" at its opening in October 1931. This eight-story structure had east and west wings which connected to a central north wing. The building was topped with a three-story dome structure and the circular room beneath was called on to serve as a ward for patients during WW II. The first appointed superintendent of the General Hospital was Dr. Hewitt in 1932.

This WW II vintage postcard is an aerial view of the Saint John General Hospital in a dull black and white composition. It is an overview of the railway valley where walls of the Stanley Street overpass can be seen while showing the residential housing of the Wright Street area. On November 1, 1982, the old General was empty; all recent patients had been moved to the new Saint John Regional Hospital facility in Millidgeville.

The former Jewett family home was first the New Brunswick School for the Deaf, until it became a soldiers' hospital in 1918. This postcard shows both the Hospital and Recreation Hut that were located at 98 Lancaster Avenue. After WW II a larger four-story brick complex known as the Department of Veterans Affairs Hospital was built. The D.V.A. was closed as a hospital in 1982 and after provincial government use, it was demolished in June of 1994.

In East Saint John, by 1930, two distinct buildings existed as hospitals on the same site and basically for the same purpose. First, the Saint John Tuberculosis Hospital, a large complex, opened on December 10, 1915 and then on February 1, 1930, the Nesbitt Memorial Wing was opened. The T.B. Hospital was a two-story brick structure located across from the Poor House on the old Red Head Road (today's Bayside Drive) facing Courtenay Bay.

The Nesbitt Memorial Wing for children was built in honor of local school teacher Andrew Nesbitt and his beloved wife by their son, Arthur J. Nesbitt. The smaller wing was in front of the larger T.B. Hospital. A trim cottage home sat between the two structures for the medical superintendent. New Brunswick children under 12 years of age were treated with good food, rest, fresh air, and sunshine at no charge.

90

One of Saint John's greatest landmarks since 1848, the Provincial Hospital, is in danger of being demolished. On February 24, 1998, the staff and patients moved to their new facility on the Ridgewood grounds in South Bay. Originally known as the Lunatic Asylum, caring for people with mental illness, it has occupied this commanding site overlooking the bridges and Reversing Falls. The now empty buildings must get new occupants within a reasonable time or their destruction will take place.

This South Bay residence, constructed from 1912 to 1915, has always been a Saint John area landmark. Built on a bluff that overlooks the St. John River, it affords a view of the bay. The imposing structure has traditionally been known as "The Castle." The 1911 newlyweds, Gladys Walker and Parker Baker, designed their dream home on Walker family property. Gladys Baker was forced to sell it in the early 1920s, yet, through many owners' hands, it still remains a private home today.

On May 1, 1922, a catastrophic fire occurred in the heart of the Fairville business district. The fire began around three o'clock in the afternoon in a house occupied by Perley Durdan, and before it was over ten buildings were consumed and four others badly damaged. Businesses destroyed included Kerrigan's Meat Market, Fairville Drug Store, Chittick's Shoe Repair, Hennessey's Dry Goods, and Stout's Furniture Store.

The New Brunswick Protestant Orphan's Home dates from its 1854 beginnings until full closure in 1979. The 45-acre landmark complex pictured here was the Quinton and Manchester properties acquired after 1923. The Manchester homestead became the Administration building in 1925 and Boys and Girls wings were built behind it. A school and an Infants' building completed the main complex. The working farm property had its buildings whose operation helped provide vegetables and milk for the orphanage until 1965.

The Raymond Hotel (1947–1972) was an early 1880s post-fire construction that was originally named the Clifton House. It offered a great panorama of the harbour from its fifth-floor cupola. A series of fires cost the hotel, when operating as the Oasis Club, step by step reductions in floors. Finally, as a three-story building, in a deteriorating state, it was demolished in the early 1990s. The lost landmark at the southwest corner of German and Princess Streets is now a parking lot.

The Armoury, built in 1911, is a city landmark that continues to serve the military presence. This two-story building has a deep basement foundation and twin complementary three-story towers at its front entrance. The central drill hall, with peaked roof, rises three stories and has been available for public functions requiring a large hall. The Armoury's grounds are located between Sydney and Wentworth Streets just off Broadview Avenue in the South End of the city.

This streetscape shows Canterbury Street from the upper corner of Church Street, southerly in a scarce postcard view. It was used for a business advertisement of the S. Hayward and Company hardware firm at 30–52 Canterbury. They operated out of this location for 37 years from 1894 to 1931. Later, O'Brien Motors, 1937–1970, created a parking garage on its upper floors. It remains a protected landmark on that street corner between King and Princess Streets.

The "Manor House," a popular hotel and tearoom located in Glen Falls, was gutted by fire on January 31, 1923. Built in 1815 by a retired British naval officer named Cudlip, it became a hotel c. 1914 after nearly a century as a private home. The Saint John Fire Department was unable to respond to the fire due to a lack of water in Glen Falls and poor road conditions.

Fourteen
SCOUTS, GUIDES, AND AUTOMOBILES

Saint John, New Brunswick, holds great transportation festival and event in Saint John, May 31-June 3, 1935.

In 1935, a number of events took place in Saint John in connection with the celebration of King George V's Silver Jubilee. By far the most grandiose was the Transportation Festival and Scout Jamboree which took place from May 31 to June 3.

The Transportation Festival was a celebration of all forms of transportation, old and new. Models of ships, planes, trains, and streetcars were all part of an elaborate set of displays at the Armoury. Of special note, the first automobile to ever appear in Saint John, a one-cylinder Rambler, was one of a number of cars on display.

At the same time, a huge Scout Jamboree was also taking place in the city. Scouts and Guides from all over the province as well as a small contingent from Maine was here to greet and honor the founder of the Scout movement, Lord Baden-Powell. Also on hand were Lady Baden-Powell and their two daughters. In our first view, the Chief Scout is just arriving at Union Station.

The Festival and Jamboree culminated with a spectacular parade that took place on the evening of June 3, the King's birthday, and included about 1,500 participants.

Saint John, New Brunswick, holds great transportation festival and scout jamboree, May 31 - June 3, 1935.

Here are Lord and Lady Baden-Powell on the day of their arrival in Saint John. They were accompanied by their daughters, Heather and Betty. As one can see at a glance, Lord Baden-Powell was much older than his wife, being nearly twice her age; he was 78 years old in this view.

Saint John, New Brunswick, holds great transportation festival and scout jamboree, May 31 - June 3, 1935.
PHOTO BY J. M. HARRISON

This photograph taken on Saturday, June 1, 1935, the day of the big Jamboree at Barrack Green, shows a portion of the three thousand Guides, Brownies, Rovers, Scouts, and Cubs who participated in the thrilling event. On the white rostrum, centre of the view, Professor James F. Browne conducted the regimental band of the Saint John Fusiliers and led the young men and women in the singing of "God Save the King," "O Canada," "My Own Canadian Home," and "A Song of Canada."

After the opening ceremonies had concluded, the Guides and Brownies broke up into smaller groups, each putting on a different display. In this shot, a group of Guides outfitted with aprons and scrubbing pails are going through a dance drill of household duties, which included scrubbing, cleaning, brushing, and mending, all done to music.

After the Guides and Brownies had finished their drills and displays, they received a command at which point they came to attention and then with a spontaneous cheer, they rushed as one to a position in front of the reviewing stand. In the view we see the Chief Guide, Lady Baden-Powell, giving her inspirational speech to the Guides and Brownies assembled before her. In her speech she urged them to "keep playing the game of Guides through your lives."

Saint John, New Brunswick, holds great transportation festival and scout jamboree, May 31–June 3, 1935.
PHOTO BY J.M. HARRISON

As the Guides and Brownies were listening to the words of their Chief, the Rovers, Scouts, and Cubs were forming up for the march past, which the Guides and Brownies also took part in. All of the various troops took part, and due to their large numbers, the march past took 45 minutes to complete. In this scene a group of flag bearers are passing by the reviewing stand with a small contingent of sea scouts both 'fore and aft.'

Saint John, New Brunswick, holds great transportation festival and

Scout leaders "face right" and salute the Chief Scout and Guide while their troop follows, carrying their crook-sticks, all eyes turned toward the honored guests. Following the Scouts are two groups of Cubs led by their own leaders and flag bearer. Every seat in the grandstand was full, and a number of young men and boys can be seen perching atop the fence in the background.

Saint John, New Brunswick, holds great transportation festival and scout jamboree, May 31–June 3, 1935.

After the march past, the Scouts and Cubs put on their big display. In addition to the bridge-building display in this view, examples of tent-pitching, friction-fire lighting, rope spinning, first aid, pyramid work, signalling in unison, and marching were performed. After the bridge was completed, Lord Baden-Powell walked across the structure to the delight of the workmen. Two Cubs, George Delaney and Douglas McCarthy, accompanied "B-P" on his inspection.

Saint John, New Brunswick, holds great transportation festival and scout jamboree, May 31–June 3, 1935.

After "B-P," as he was affectionately known, had returned to the stand, he was also complimented with a "field rush" as young men crowded in front of the grandstand. He started to talk several times but was drowned out by sustained cheering. Finally with a crisp "Good lads," he brought them to attention. He expressed how happy he was to see them all, commended them for their performance and urged them to continue in the scouting movement with the ultimate goal of "universal peace."

Saint John, New Brunswick, holds great transportation festival and scout jamboree, May 31–June 3, 1935.

On Sunday, June 2, the day after the Jamboree, some 1,500 members of the Boy Scout movement in New Brunswick paraded Saint John streets on their way to various church services. In this view on Charlotte Street, Lt.-Gov. Murray MacLaren, with Lady Baden-Powell behind, accepts the salute from passing Cubs, Scouts, and Rovers. "B-P" did not attend the parade, needing to rest after Saturday's strenuous program.

Saint John, New Brunswick, holds great transportation festival and ...

This view was taken Monday, June 3, the day of the great "March of Transportation" parade. It began at 7 a.m. with the various bands, other marching units and floats beginning on Charlotte Street and proceeding up to King Square, turning down King Street, through Market Square and up Dock Street on their way to the North End, Mount Pleasant and back to the city centre. Here we see the band of the Saint John Fusiliers passing by the reviewing stand at Market Square.

Saint John, New Brunswick, holds great transportation festival and scout jamboree, May 31-June 3, 1935.

On the reviewing stand at Market Square, Lt.-Gov. MacLaren, second from left, took the salute of the marching units. Joining him were several dignitaries and other honored guests, including Lady Baden-Powell and her daughter Betty, Mayor Brittain, Premier Tilley, Chief Justice J.B.M. Baxter, and several officers from the USS *Macdonough*, a United States destroyer commanded by Commander Charles S. Alden, which was visiting the port during the celebrations.

Saint John, New Brunswick, holds great transportation festival and scout jamboree, May 31-June 3, 1935.

Following a "modern" fire truck are several of the commercial floats. Directly behind was the float of S. McCormick's Grocery, located at 10 Main Street in Fairville. The third float in line represented another more familiar Fairville business, that of T.S. Simms & Co. Ltd. Atop the float was a model of the large brush factory at Fairville Corner, now known to most as Simms Corner.

The first three vehicles in this view are unidentified. However, next in line was a modern delivery truck representing G.B. Taylor's North End pork-packing business, which was located at 200 Bridge Street. Behind Taylor's truck is thought to be the float of Parker D. Mitchell, Ltd. Their entry was a cream and green coloured model home heated by an automatic stoker with a display of coal of various types. Mitchell's was then located on the West Side waterfront at 1 Water Street.

This is the end of the parade at Market Square. The horse-drawn truck and the modern delivery truck behind it belonged to West Side Dairies. Aboard the float were farmers playing old-time dance music. Notice the Primrose (later Irving) gas station in the background. On the second floor directly above the sign, a man in a white shirt can be seen watching the parade from his office window. That man is purported to be none other than Kenneth Colin Irving.

102

Fifteen
BUSINESSES

This chapter will show interesting landmark spaces where Saint Johners worked in refining and manufacturing jobs, found lodging, shopped, paid bills, looked after health needs, ate meals, created artistic works, and served the tourist trade.

The best way to pay homage to our strongest business elements of the community, the Irving Family, is to show its oil products' flagship headquarters under construction in 1931. The Golden Ball building at the corner of 244 Union and Sydney Street remains a main nerve centre within the Irving Empire in a shared role with the nearby SMT building, which headquarters the forestry business.

This photograph of the six-story construction highlights two era contrasts to one of Saint John's first modern 20th-century business towers. They are, first, the sloven on Sydney Street parked at the curb and then the cobblestoned road at King Square North and Sydney Street.

Gurd's Bottling Plant was built on the former site of the Victoria Rink at 189 City Road in 1928. Their Maritime branch produced ginger ales and carbonated beverages in glass bottles that are avidly sought by local collectors. When the business closed in 1941, Saint John Milling Co. took over the plant and continued producing flour until 1968. Most of the vacant mill was torn down when the Colonial Inn developed the site in 1972. Gurd's original structure, pictured, was kept as the Inn's offices.

Opened in 1928 as the Riviera Tea Room, this restaurant located at 91 Charlotte Street quickly became a local institution. The Riviera had a classy look with an atmosphere that was informal while serving fare that was excellent. Many city organizational groups met at this restaurant, where their banquet areas amply provided for noon lunch meetings. Business ceased in 1985; later an unexpected explosion and fire caused by a gas leak on an early Saturday morning, April 19, 1986, completely destroyed the vacant restaurant.

Going for a coke at "The Riv?" This was the most posed question of the day for high school students throughout this landmark's existence. Co-author Terry Keleher has vivid memories of being a 12-year-old, independently treating himself to a planned Saturday afternoon travelling from the West Side "over town." It included a bus trip, lunch, and a movie. "The Riv" was the high point, where he usually dined on a coke and hot chicken sandwich and trimmings for $1.25.

The Paradise Restaurant at 85 Charlotte Street opened in 1923. Originally it was the Paradise Ice Cream Parlour, and later it became the Tropical Paradise, but in all cases, it was the Paradise. Never in the same class as the Riviera, it provided Saint Johners with quick lunch counter fare in comfortable booths. It ceased operations in 1964.

Thomas Stockwell Simms embarked in the brush-making business in 1866. For 126 years T.S. Simms has maintained a business in Saint John. Their present plant at Simms Corner was completed on "Suspension Bridge Rd., Fairville." Its construction over 1911–12 created many city firsts and also changed the way employees laboured in their modern working environment. The huge, all-concrete structure was a first, standing four stories high, 52 feet wide, and 400 feet long with a 150-foot chimney.

The Simms manufacturing plant opened in 1913 with a 1,000-gallon water pump reservoir creating the city's first sprinkler system. It was a bright, airy, and healthy environment provided in part due to the 25,000 glass window panes. Workers, because of the long distance for most to their workplace, now could use the plant lunchroom, which was very unusual for that time. Wash basins providing both hot and cold running water was another first for this well-established firm.

The Corona Company Ltd., a branch of the Ganong Brothers, the famous chocolate candy company of St. Stephen, was created in 1913. Ganong's definitely had a hands-on operation with the youngest brother, Walter, in charge until 1922. However, the prime purpose was to dissuade other large candy competitors from establishing in Saint John. The plant, at 277–293 Union Street, also used equipment from the former White Candy Company, 240–244 Union Street, which ceased their operations in 1912.

Corona Chocolates

**Pure materials
blended under
Hygienic
conditions.**

Mfrd. under A. S. Spiegel's Patents, Series B, for The Kenyon Company, Des Moines, Iowa

BEND TO AND FRO

The Corona Company, Limited,
ST. JOHN, CANADA.

Ganong's felt that "White's" name had "bad repute" in Saint John, so they called the company Corona. Corona, with 150 to two hundred employees, produced Dorothy Kingston chocolates, so named because the Ganongs came from the Kingston Peninsula originally. By 1932, Corona had served its purpose well, but now was more of a liability; therefore, Ganong's ceased its operations. The candy production lines were relocated in St. Stephen and the Corona plant continued as a storage facility until 1950.

In March of 1914 the Atlantic Sugar Refinery buildings were almost completed. The City of Saint John had provided their 7-acre tract of land at the eastern side of the mouth of the harbour. By February 18, 1915 the plant started melting raw sugar and has continued doing so for the past 83 years, while employing up to 800 workers in the earlier years. Lantic Sugar is a soft sugar product in great demand.

Longtime residents of Saint John will no doubt remember the dry goods business of F.W. Daniel & Co. that was a fixture at the corner of Charlotte and King Streets from 1910 to 1951. F.W. Daniel's is featured in this c. 1930 view. Note the traffic policeman at the head of King Street (perhaps Andy Duffy?) and the woman about to board a westbound streetcar just before it turns down King.

In 1882, Max Ungar opened a laundry business at 301/2 Waterloo Street. Ungar's Laundry became a fixture there, expanding in size to eventually occupy 28–40 Waterloo before closing in 1958. Next door at 24 Waterloo, Jules Grondines, a gold and silversmith, opened a plating business in 1906 and incredibly he remained in business there until 1975.

C.H.S.J. Radio went on the air in 1934 and continues today. This 1945 postcard promoted both the station and our talented local group, the Maritime Farmers. They played for another 20 years and their fiddle tunes in the country and western style had a large following. Today, respected banjo player and singer George Hector and great fiddler Ned Landry continue to play. Both men and Harvey Wayne are in New Brunswick's Country Music Hall of Fame.

W. Tremaine Gard & Son, watchmakers and jewellers, was located at 51 Charlotte Street corner South Market, in the City Market Building, from 1932 until it closed in 1953. This firm was established in 1870, and from this location the business was being managed by his son, L. Tremaine Gard. Besides the main floor shown in the postcard it had an additional second floor showroom for china. Today, Billy's Seafood Company occupies that location.

F.W. Woolworth's 5¢, 10¢ and 15¢ department store at 93–97 King Street, which opened in 1912 and closed in 1993, was a beloved landmark at the corner of King and Charlotte Streets. When the F.W. Daniel & Co. store closed in 1951, after 40 years, Woolworth's quickly occupied their space and by 1952 had created a modern new complex. Woolworth's operated from that location between King and South Market Streets for about 40 years.

Sixteen

OTHER SPORTS

Since 1785, Saint John has always had a marvelous tradition in sporting events, in particular those that involved water. Worthy of special mention are the Paris Crew, the four-man World Rowing Champions of the 1860s and 1870s.

This postcard shows the Sailing Yacht *Canada*, which is the oldest registered yacht in the Canadian Shipping Registry. In storage for nearly 30 years, restoration has begun so that she may ply the waters again.

The Yacht *Canada* was launched into Saint John Harbour in the spring of 1898. It was designed by James McIntyre of Boston, Massachusetts and constructed by William Heans Sr. for his son Fred and two friends, Howard Holder and Howard Camp. Within a few years, Fred Heans became the sole owner.

The Yacht *Canada* was the fastest boat of her size and class up until the First World War. She won over 40 major racing trophies when she was skippered by the Heans family. The Yacht *Canada* and the Royal Kennebeccasis Yacht Club, the club the yacht raced out of, are marking their 100th anniversaries in 1998.

The Yacht *Canada* is undergoing a complete refurbishing for her projected re-launch in the summer of 2000, in Ontario on the Rideau River. This is being done through the valiant efforts of a dedicated group of volunteers who continue to raise monies under the Sailing Yacht *Canada* Restoration Project.

In 1898, the Saint John Yacht Club became the Royal Kennebeccasis Yacht Club by Royal Charter granted by Queen Victoria. This year marks its centennial as the R.K.Y.C., one of Canada's oldest sailing clubs that has a long tradition of speedy craft in various classes. We introduced the R.K.Y.C. clubhouse in our first book and we felt on its 100th anniversary, this patriotic postcard of the R.K.Y.C. Commodore's Yacht marks a history that continues today with Commodore David Weyman.

Pictured above is the St. John High School basketball team, Provincial and Maritime champions for 1922–23. Undefeated at home and losers of only two games the entire season, they defeated Colchester Academy from Nova Scotia 24–9 to win the Maritime title. The members, from left to right, are as follows: (sitting) M. Ewing (sub.), W. Donohoe (forward and captain), F. Campbell (guard and manager), and E. Gunn (sub.); (standing) D. MacLauchlan (guard), R. Shaw (coach), H. Humphrey (center), and A. Wittrien (forward).

Here is the 1925 New Brunswick Intermediate Football Champion Fairville Canucks. The Canucks went undefeated throughout the 1925 season, culminating with a 5–0 victory over the Nationals to win the Harding Cup in the championship final, which was played on the Sand Cove Road grounds on November 28. The winning touchdown was scored by R. Sherwood and was converted by H. Peters. Among the players on the team was Ed Snodgrass (seated, second from right), one of Saint John's premier speedskaters.

This was the 1926–27 St. Vincent's Boys High School Basketball Team. Located on Cliff Street from 1919 to 1954, this Catholic school then moved into a new building at St. Malachy's High on Sydney Street. In 1976, St. Malachy's became co-ed. They are from left to right: (front row) J. Kirk (forward, capt.) and M. Dolan (forward); (middle row) B. Dwyer (defense), R. Lawlor (center), and G. Sheehan (defense); (back row) W. King (defense), W. E. Stirling (coach), and D. Kirk (forward).

This is a marvellous group shot of the East End Playground with Rockwood Park's hills in the background. It was located off Rothesay Avenue and bordered Marsh Creek where today's Post Office Complex is located. The Saint John Playground Association officially began in 1912, and these four photographs covering both pages came from the A.M. Belding estate. Mr. Belding was the editor of the *Evening Times Globe* and served as secretary of the Playground Association that inaugural year.

The young ladies are playing basketball and the hoop is just above the heads of that tight knot of girls. The backs of the houses that would front the Marsh Road can be seen. This field was the Saint John Cricket Club grounds in the 1870s and the Saint John Athletic Club grounds by the late 1880s. Later, in an 1895 merger, it became the B. and A. grounds when the Saint John Bicycle and Athletic Clubs amalgamated.

This photograph was very likely of that initial year's Opening Day Ceremony, judging by how well the children and their gentleman playground leader are dressed. All four photos were taken on the same day as were others that were not used. A spirited game of girls field hockey catches the playground leader in his referee's role. The young ladies, some in large bonnets, are all wearing full dresses.

The boys shine at the high jumping exhibition on this opening day. The girls are spectators for this sport. Behind the fence winds Marsh Creek, and this photograph was taken facing east out the Marsh Valley. A later newspaper playgrounds listing in 1930 describes the East End Playground as being located beyond the Marsh Bridge. Saint John continues to have a great playground program and there is no doubt that many fine young sports persons developed on their playgrounds.

This photograph shows Hilton Belyea in a speedskating outfit in 1923, ready for a Seniors' race. Belyea won the New England single sculls rowing championship in 1921, stunning the race scene by setting a world record at 37 years of age in the 1.5 mile with turn distance. Belyea went on to capture both the 1921 and 1922 Canadian Championships. A 1924 Olympic row netted a special medal, and Belyea retired at 42 in 1927.

Beginning in the 1930s, J. Fred (Bollard) Belyea operated a skating rink in back of his three houses at #1 through #5 Ludlow Street West. There was a small charge for evening skating to music on the lighted surface. A place to put on skates was a back porch or vacant apartment. This 1935 photograph shows three girls, left to right, Lois Vaughan, Catherine Vaughan, and Eileen Chase. Hilton Belyea, J. Fred's younger brother, had a rink some years earlier on the millpond.

In the fall of 1914, Rothesay Collegiate School played football (rugby) in a league with two other teams—Saint John High School and Fredericton High School. Every team played a four game schedule, two at home and two away. This R.C.S. First Football (Rugby) Team shown played well, winning two, losing two and, in effect, ending up in second place to winning team Saint John High School.

This Saint John Beavers Hockey Team of 1946–47 was coming off a great season winning the 1946 Maritime Senior Hockey Championship. Largely through Bill Giggey's brilliant goal tending, they upset the favored Halifax Navy team. Most of their players had returned and their new additions like Nick Nicolle were extremely capable. Jackie Keating remained as coach and they played in the new Big Four League with Moncton Hawks, Truro Bearcats, and Halifax Crescents. That 1947 season was to be the Hawks' year.

The Riverside Golf and Country Club is located in East Riverside beside the Kennebecasis River and it hosted the 1939 Canadian Open, and a number of postcards captured the event. This postcard shows tournament play on one of the greens for the $3,000 in total prize money. A New Brunswick course was considered well off the beaten track and a great many of the name players passed on this open and its $1,000 winner's prize money.

This postcard shows the 18th hole with the Club House behind where H. (Jug) McSpaden of Winchester, Massachusetts was the winner. His rounds of 67, 69, 73, and 73 gave him a grand total of 282, five under his nearest competitor. Earle Jamieson, the Digby Pines Pro, won the special prize for Maritime Pros, shooting rounds of 81, 83, 87, and 75 for a total of 325, giving him $5.

Seventeen
ROYAL AND OFFICIAL CELEBRATIONS

Saint John, N.B. celebrates the Silver Jubilee of the accession of

The ten year period from 1929 to 1939 saw a number of official events and celebrations, both royal and otherwise, which took place in Saint John. In addition to the Scout Jamboree and Transportation Festival of 1935, the list of events includes the 1929 dedication of the Studholme Cairn at Fort Howe, the 1934 New Brunswick sesquicentennial which included the opening of the New Brunswick Museum on Douglas Avenue, additional 1935 George V Silver Jubilee celebrations, and the 1939 Royal Visit of King George VI and Queen Elizabeth.

Among the events that took place during the 1935 George V Silver Jubilee celebrations was a colorful military church parade on May 5. L.M. Harrison produced this real-photo postcard of the Saint John Fusiliers Band as they marched along Sydney Street. Other bands participating in the parade were those of the 3rd New Brunswick Medium Brigade and the R.C.N.V.R. pipers.

Saint John, N.B. celebrates the Silver Jubilee of the accession of King George V to the throne May 6, 1935

Following the church parade, the various units assembled on King Street East by the Loyalist Cemetery at a point opposite the old Central Police Station. The men formed a hollow square within which Lt. Gov. Murray MacLaren made efficiency and long service medal presentations to a group of 12 men. In this view, he is shown presenting the Canadian Efficiency Decoration to Lt. Col. Gordon G.K. Holder, D.C.M., M.M., officer commanding the Saint John Fusiliers.

On the evening of May 6, 1935, the Boy Scouts staged a nationwide Silver Jubilee celebration by lighting bonfires in cities, towns, and villages across Canada. The bonfires were symbolic "beacons" of loyalty to the King. This is the "Fort Howe Beacon" while others were located at Martello Tower hill and Blacks Point. About five thousand in attendance also witnessed the firing of 21 rockets that released stars of green, gold, and red (Scout colors), before the fire was lit.

Here seated in this photograph are the official dedication group who are installing Fort Howe as a national site with a monument on September 11, 1929. Standing and chairing the event is Dr. Clarence Webster; to his right, blocked out by papers is Mayor White of Saint John; to his left Maj. Gen. Hugh McLean, New Brunswick's lieutenant governor; Brig. Gen. F.W. Hill, Officer Commanding Dist. No. 7 in New Brunswick; and Vice Admiral Sir Cyril T.M. Fuller, Officer Commanding the British North American Squadron.

This postcard shows Brig. Gen. Hill at the cairn addressing the crowd before unveiling the bronze plaque that details Major Studholme's illustrious career, beginning from 1776 when he helped quell a rebellion at Chignecto. Studholme had Fort Howe constructed in 1778 and was its commander. He drove off American raiders during the Revolutionary War and helped prevent an Indian uprising. Studholme acted as Crown Agent when the Loyalists arrived in Saint John in 1783, giving them assistance in settlement.

On August 16, 1934, the first day of the New Brunswick sesquicentennial celebrations at Saint John, an impressive and colourful military ceremony took place on the exhibition grounds at Barrack Green. The "Trooping" of their former colours by the Saint John Fusiliers (26th Batt. C.E.F.) took place in front of a large gathering, which included Prime Minister R.B. Bennett. A portion of the old Exhibition building, destroyed by fire in 1941, can be seen in the upper left corner.

Part of the two-day New Brunswick sesquicentennial celebrations in Saint John was the unveiling of the monument in King Square dedicated to the founders of the province on August 17, 1934. Taking part in this ceremony was the famous 48th Highlanders Band from Toronto, shown here with the old courthouse in the background. The tall man on the left was Drum Major J. Small and to his left the commanding officer, Pipe Major James R. Fraser.

122

On Thursday, August 16, 1934, as part of New Brunswick's sesquicentennial celebrations, the official opening of Douglas Avenue's New Brunswick Museum took place at 3 p.m. Many distinguished guests were on the steps of the museum as Prime Minister R.B. Bennett, who opened the museum, is seen addressing the crowd. It was a great day with sports events and band concerts through the afternoon and a huge parade that evening.

On June 13, 1939, King George VI and his wife Queen Elizabeth visited Saint John as part of their Canadian tour that year. Here, the Royal procession is about to turn onto Prince William Street from the foot of King. The Royal couple were on their way to Barrack Green where a reception took place that included over ten thousand school children.

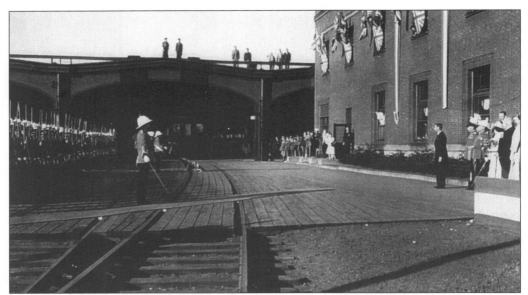

From Barrack Green the King and Queen proceeded to Union Station where they would depart for Moncton. The Royal party is shown on the right as the Guard of Honor (Saint John Fusiliers) presents arms to Their Majesties. In front of the guard nearest the camera is Captain G.C. Wilson, commander of the guard, and beyond him is Second Lieutenant James Wattling, dipping the King's colour in a Royal salute.

This is a rooftop view of the Honor Guard at Union Station. In front, Second Lieutenant Wattling holds the King's colours while behind the guard the Fusiliers band stands ready as members of the Canadian Legion, B.E.S.L., take their places. Behind them, members of the public gathered hoping for a last look at the Royal visitors.

Eighteen

WORLD WAR II

RECREATION ROOM FOR ARMED SERVICES AND MERCHANT NAVY.
CARLETON BR. NO. 2 CANADIAN LEGION, WEST SAINT JOHN. N. B.

During the 1930s, Saint John, like the rest of North America was caught in the throes of a lengthy Depression. Nobody wanted war when it came in 1939, but it did have the effect of resurrecting the economies of both Canada and the United States. Saint John was no exception as it returned to full employment for the first time since WW I. There was the increased presence of the military, building and repairing of ships, countless industries producing goods needed for the war effort, and the resultant spin-offs of all this activity.

The organization that bonds all of Canada's military veterans and their families is the Royal Canadian Legion, formed in 1926, known as the Canadian Legion of the British Empire Service League until 1962. The first New Brunswick branch of the Legion to receive its charter was Carleton No. 2, located in West Saint John. This branch met for many years in the old Carleton City Hall, now the Carleton Community Centre, the location of the view on this *c.* 1940s postcard.

Above is a postcard of Martello Tower that was produced just prior to the beginning of WW II. Although still owned by the military, it had been basically a tourist attraction since before the turn of the century. Shortly after Canada declared war against Germany the tower, designated as a Fire Command Post in June 1939, became the site of an anti-aircraft battery.

This is a view of Martello Tower as it appeared after WW II. The two-story cement structure added to the tower served as the Fire Command Post. A number of temporary structures were constructed nearby to serve as administrative buildings. Today, only the tower remains, virtually unchanged over the past 50 years.

By far the most prolific producer of Saint John postcards during WW II was the Photogelatine Engraving Company of Ottawa. Their cards typically featured low-quality picture reproduction, which is evident in this view of King Street, c. 1940. Notice how traffic is bearing to the extreme right side of the street in order to leave the tracks clear for the then aging streetcars.

During the Second World War, as in the first, scrap metal became a precious commodity. Just how precious it was is evident in this shot of the bandstand in King Square. People were encouraged to donate their old pots and pans to the war effort to be used in the manufacture of ammunition, weapons, vehicles, etc. Among the banners placed on the bandstand was one that read, "Take a pot shot at Hitler."

In 1936, the New Brunswick Power Company, who owned and operated the streetcars in Saint John, began using busses on a limited basis. By 1943, the busses were beginning to take over from the old streetcars that would come to the end of the line in 1948. This wartime shot taken at Market Square (current location of city hall) shows a Power Company bus which, in addition to carrying its passengers, is being used as a rolling billboard.

A military band purported to be that of No. 4 Garrison marching south on Charlotte Street in the summer of 1945. Much has changed since then. The buildings containing the Riviera Restaurant and the Empire Shoe Rebuilders were destroyed by explosions and fire in 1986 following a gas leak that caused the evacuation of much of the uptown area. The remainder of buildings were demolished in the early 1980s to make way for the Royal Bank building that now occupies the site.